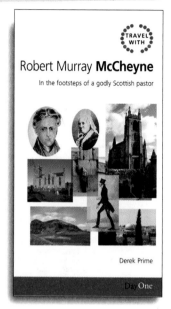

TRAVEL WITH

Robert Murray **McCheyne**

In the footsteps of a godly Scottish pastor

Derek Prime

Day One

Series Editor: Brian H Edwards

Day One

Robert **Murray McCheyne**

Meet Robert Murray McCheyne

'Too good to be true' was my reaction when I first heard people speak of McCheyne. Gifted as a student, pastor, teacher, poet, hymn-writer, and artist—so much was complimentary. This meant that I read biographies of him with a degree of scepticism. However, the more I read the more I was convinced of the value of his godly influence and the enriching qualities of his example.

Robert Murray McCheyne died at the age of twenty-nine, yet the record of his life and ministry has had a remarkable impact upon the Christian church worldwide and it is appropriate to ask why, particularly because that influence is greater now than when he lived. Biographies continue to be written and his example and writings quoted.

McCheyne served God at a strategic time in the life of the church in Scotland when many significant changes were taking place. He taught his people to pray for revival, but when it came, he himself was away in Palestine. The news and subsequent recording of the revival was important in encouraging many elsewhere to cry for similar blessing from God—this was undoubtedly answered in 1839.

The records of McCheyne's life are based mainly on his diary and journal in which he frankly expressed his feelings and experiences. The young pastor can have had little or no idea that what he wrote would be published and read by others. Most significantly, McCheyne made a lasting impression upon his contemporaries. Andrew Bonar, his closest friend, wrote, 'All who knew him not only saw in him a burning and a shining light, but felt also the breathing of the hidden life of God.'

His influence upon evangelicalism has certainly been underestimated. He has been described as one of the 'overlooked shapers of evangelicalism'.

Pictured: Robert Murray McCheyne Drawn by himself and found in a little pocket note-book relating to the year 1843

---

amateur. This led him—as was often done in such cases—to ask the Presbytery of Edinburgh, under whose superintendence he had carried on his studies, to transfer the remainder of his public trials to another Presbytery, where there would be less pressure of business to cause delay. This request was readily granted and his connection with Dumfriesshire led him to the Presbytery of Annan, the district from which his mother came. Further probationary sermons had to be preached and he was required to submit five linguistic and homiletical assignments. His examination proved satisfactory, and having signed the Confession of Faith, he was licensed 'to preach the gospel of our Lord and Saviour Jesus Christ as a probationer for the holy ministry.' This meant that he could preach but not dispense the sacraments. He could now look for a call to a church and then ordination would take place.

After being licensed on 1 July 1835, McCheyne's first sermons were preached at Ruthwell the following Sunday. In the evening he spoke on 'The Pool of Bethesda', and in the afternoon on 'The Strait Gate'. He wrote in his diary: 'Found a view awfully solemn thing than I had imagined, to announce Christ authoritatively; yet a glorious privilege!'

EDINBURGH

1 EDINBURGH CASTLE
2 CANONGATE
3 CANONGATE CHURCH
4 JOHN KNOX'S
5 THE PALACE OF HOLYROOD
6 HOLYROOD PARK
7 ARTHUR'S SEAT

8 GLADSTONE'S LAND
9 THE PEOPLE'S STORY
10 THE SCOTTISH PARLIAMENT
11 THE GRANGE CEMETERY
12 ST CATHERINE'S ARGYLE CHURCH

TRAVEL INFORMATION

Edinburgh Castle

The Castle is at the top of the Royal Mile (www.edinburghcastle.gov.uk) and located approx at the summit. The Castle is the main symbol of Edinburgh's landmarks and each year hosts the world-renowned Edinburgh Military Tattoo. It also has a place of defence for the city since 1085. It has also served in the past as a prison.

Canongate

This is at the Holyrood Abbey and of the Mile and it takes its name from the canons that once ran the abbey at Holyrood and it was an independent burgh from Edinburgh from 1128 to 1636. 'Gate' in Scots means 'way' or 'street'.

Canongate church

Built in the 1680s, the churchyard contains the graves of some famous people. Of particular interest is the memorial to Horatius Bonar, one of McCheyne's friends and the writer of many hymns, including 'I heard the voice of Jesus say.'

The Palace of Holyroodhouse

Established as a monastery in 1128, the Palace of Holyroodhouse is the official Scottish residence of the Royal Family. It is used for state ceremonies and its gardens for royal garden parties. When the sovereign is not in residence, it is open to visitors. Details are found

Above: Ruthwell Church where McCheyne preached his first sermon as a probationer minister on 1 July 1835

CONTENTS

A CIP record is held at The British Library   ISBN 978 1 84625 0576

Published by Day One Publications Ryelands Road, Leominster, HR6 8NZ

01568 613 740 FAX 01568 611 473   email: sales@dayone.co.uk www.dayone.co.uk   All rights reserved

part of this publication may be reproduced, or stored in a retrieval system, or transmitted, in any form or by any means,
mechanical, electronic, photocopying, recording or otherwise, without the prior permission of Day One Publications

Design and Art Direction: Steve Devane Printed by Gutenberg Press, Malta

Dedication: To Cilla who, like McCheyne, found Dundee a special place

Meet Robert Murray McCheyne

'Too good to be true' was my reaction when I first heard people speak of McCheyne. Gifted as a student, pastor, teacher, poet, hymn-writer, and artist—so much was complimentary. This meant that I read biographies of him with a degree of scepticism. However, the more I read the more I was convinced of the value of his godly influence and the enriching qualities of his example.

Robert Murray McCheyne died at the age of twenty-nine, but the record of his life and ministry has had a remarkable impact upon the Christian church worldwide and it is appropriate to ask why, particularly because that influence is greater now than when he lived. Biographies continue to be written and his example and writings quoted.

McCheyne served God at a strategic time in the life of the church in Scotland when many significant changes were taking place. He taught his people to pray for revival, but when it came, he himself was away in Palestine. The news and subsequent recording of the revival was important in encouraging many elsewhere to cry for similar blessing from God—this was undoubtedly answered in 1859.

The records of McCheyne's life are based mainly on his diary and journal in which he frankly expressed his feelings and experiences. The young pastor can have had little or no idea that what he wrote would be published and read by others. Most significantly, McCheyne made a lasting impression upon his contemporaries. Andrew Bonar, his closest friend, wrote, 'All who knew him not only saw in him a burning and a shining light, but felt also the breathing of the hidden life of God.'

His influence upon evangelicalism has certainly been underestimated. He has been described as one of the 'overlooked shapers of evangelicalism'.

Facing page: Robert Murray McCheyne drawn by himself and found in a little pocket notebook relating to the year 1843

❶ Pleasant places and attractive prospects

Brought up in Edinburgh, one of the most attractive cities of Europe, Robert Murray McCheyne had family roots in the west of Scotland, not far from the border with England. A stable family, a famous school and eminent teachers were to stand him in good stead

Both Robert's parents came from the southwest of Scotland and moved to Edinburgh only after their marriage. His father, Adam McCheyne, born in 1781, was brought up in a small village called Penpont, in the valley of the Scaur Water, two miles (3.2 km) west of Thornhill in the region of Dumfries and Galloway. About 16 miles (25.7 km) north of the better-known town of Dumfries, the village has the distinction of being the birthplace in 1856 of the famous geologist and explorer Joseph Thomson, and the inventor of the bicycle Kirkpatrick Macmillan, a blacksmith, born nearby in 1813. Adam McCheyne had three brothers, the eldest of whom was a lieutenant in the 64th Regiment of Foot, and the other two were a stonedyker (he built dry-stone walls) and a gardener. His gardener brother's total estate when he died was valued at four shillings and two pence, an indication of the humble nature of the family background. As the youngest son in the family, Adam may well have managed to go to university through the financial

Facing page: Ruthwell Church where McCheyne preached his first sermon in 1835

Top: Ruthwell Manse in the 19th century. It was in the garden here that McCheyne enjoyed gymnastics whilst on holiday as a boy

Above: Ruthwell Manse today, most recently a hotel

support of his older brothers, which was a common practice.

Robert's mother's maiden name was Lockhart Murray Dickson, and she was the youngest of nine children. Her background was socially and financially superior to that of her husband and she was some nine years older. Her father owned the prosperous estate of Nether Locharwood in the parish of Ruthwell and the family probably looked more favourably upon the marriage than they might otherwise have done because Adam was a young law-student, soon to establish himself in the nation's capital. Ruthwell was to be a favourite holiday place for Robert throughout his childhood, with many happy associations, not least horse riding and gymnastics in the garden of the parish minister.

Once they were married in

Above: James Ritchie & Son, still in business since the time of McCheyne

November 1802, it was natural for Adam and Lockhart to move to Edinburgh, for that was where all the action was for young lawyers hoping for the prospect of advancement; with a rapidly growing population, it was also the fashionable place to be. Edinburgh's expansion prompted imaginative and exciting building

Above: Regent Terrace, Edinburgh, designed by the eminent architect William Playfair in 1820, who earned the city the title 'the Athens of the North'

Above: Inside the Signet Library, Edinburgh

programmes, and the architect William Playfair earned Edinburgh the title of 'the Athens of the North'. Robert's mother must have appreciated Edinburgh's lively shops, compared with those of rather sleepy Dumfriesshire. Although designed originally as a residential street, Princes Street was at this time being converted into shops. No doubt she frequented the shop of Robert Shepherd, the largest grocers in Edinburgh at 83 South Bridge, and the busy fruit market gathered round the Tron; she perhaps bought a watch or clock at James Ritchie's in Leith Street, a firm still in business.

Once established in Edinburgh, Adam McCheyne trained for, and became in 1814, a member of the Society of Writers to His Majesty's Signet. This immediately increased the family's social status. The Society of Writers to Her Majesty's Signet is based in the Signet Library at the heart of the historic Old Town of Edinburgh; it is situated in Parliament Square in the shadow of St Giles Cathedral. King George IV described the library as 'the finest drawing room in Europe' and Adam McCheyne saw the opening of the building in 1822. As a Writer to the Signet, he conducted cases through the Court of Session and prepared legal documents such as crown writs and charters. His professional work introduced him to people of prominence and influence, producing rich financial dividends. This is evidenced by the addresses in Edinburgh's New Town at which he lived— 14 Dublin Street, 56 Queen Street and 20 Hill Street—all of which remain today.

Affectionate, active and artistic

Robert was born at 14 Dublin Street on 21 May 1813, the youngest of five children. A sister, Isabella, died eighteen months before his birth when she was only four months old and Eliza, his other sister who never married, was to be especially close to Robert later in his life. His eldest brother David became a lawyer like his father, and his other brother William entered medicine, becoming a surgeon with the East India Company. David had the greatest influence upon Robert because of his godly example and spiritual concern for him. The Queen Street house was the family home during the years of McCheyne's education at school and university and seems to have been the favourite home with its spacious rooms and its easy view of the Firth of Forth and the shores of Fife. The landlord's unsatisfactory care of the property prompted the move to 20 Hill Street.

As in most families one child tends to be the liveliest, and Robert bore that character in his family. He was described as affectionate, amenable, tidy, active and artistic. He was eminently teachable, although not precocious, since at the age of four he could write the Greek alphabet from memory, something accomplished when he was recovering from an illness. He displayed a great sense of fun and enjoyed physical activity. Family holidays were usually spent with his mother's family in Ruthwell,

Left: 14 Dublin Street where Robert was born in 1813. Dublin Street was one of the most fashionable addresses in the nineteenth century

Above: The Savings Bank Museum, Ruthwell

most often staying with a maiden aunt at her farm in Clarencefield close by. Ruthwell had the advantages of both the country and the seaside and it was there that his appreciation and love of nature began and grew. A letter home to his brother William in Edinburgh describes his boyish delight in the animals on the farm: three swine; two sows; seven pigs; eight hens, no cock; eight ducks, two drakes; one goose; one gander; one mare, one blood-mare (a famous rider); one filly; two cats; one canary; four cows; three heifers or bullocks and a bee-hive. The skill he gained in riding served him well later on when, as an assistant in Larbert and a minister in Dundee, he went about his pastoral duties on his pony named 'Tully'.

While in Ruthwell frequent visits were made to the parish manse where all the children affectionately called Henry Duncan, the minister, 'Uncle'. From all accounts, he must have been a fascinating character because not only was he the minister of the parish but also the founder of the first savings bank. McCheyne loved the gymnastics in the garden, and also the evening get-togethers in the manse when there was 'singing and spouting and I don't know what all.' Holiday visits to Ruthwell continued into McCheyne's late teens and his delight in it was seen in the various sketches he drew.

An outstanding school

Between the ages of five and six Robert began his education in the English School in Edinburgh—a school run by Mr George Knight—in which he excelled in recitation, showing himself to have both a quick ear and a melodious voice. After a couple of years he moved to the High School, now known as the Royal High, where he was a pupil from 1821–1827. The origins of the

**Henry Duncan
(1774–1846)**

Having moved from Scotland to England to work for a brief period in Liverpool at Heywood's Bank, Henry Duncan returned to Scotland to train for the ministry and accepted the parish of Ruthwell, where he worked for nearly half a century. Besides the attraction of the Solway that drew him, he was challenged by the social and spiritual needs of the rural communities of Scotland. He revived a failing Friendly Society in the village so that it flourished. He supplied flax to the women to encourage cottage industry and employed their husbands in turning the manse glebe of 50 acres into a superb garden. He was instrumental in the building of a Society Room that became a focal meeting point for the village as well as the birthplace of the first Savings Bank in 1810, upon which others were modelled. The University of St Andrews awarded him the honorary degree of Doctor of Divinity. Besides all this, he was a geologist, a gardener and farmer, a founder of newspapers and an artist. As a minister he inspired McCheyne by his combination of scholarship, pastoral care and evangelical zeal.

Above: Henry Duncan the minister at Ruthwell, known as 'Uncle' to the McCheyne children

school go back to the beginning of the 16th century. It was a tremendously popular school with a growing roll; besides boys from England and Ireland, others came from Russia, Germany, Switzerland, the United States, Barbados, St Vincent, Demerara and the East Indies. James Boswell, a former pupil of the school, spoke so highly of it to the famous Dr Johnston that the latter was compelled 'to confess that the High School of Edinburgh did well'. By the time Robert attended the school it had a history of gifted achievers—and was to produce many more. Sir Walter Scott was a pupil in the school from 1779; Thomas Stevenson (father of Robert Louis Stevenson) though five years younger than McCheyne, joined the school before Robert left.

What distinguished the school from many others in Edinburgh was its control by the Town Council rather than the church presbytery. It was one of three Edinburgh schools that existed to teach Latin Grammar in order to prepare boys of between eight and fourteen for entry to the universities. It was only in the mid 20th century that a classical language—Latin or Greek—ceased to be a requirement for entry to Oxford and Cambridge. The school reached its maximum enrolment in 1820, the year before Robert began. The High School reckoned on a school career of six years, with the last two years in the Rector's class. The School consisted of five classes or forms, with the fifth or highest class assigned to the Rector, in which

Left: The old High School building, where Robert attended from 1821–1827, now used by Edinburgh University for the Department of Archaeology. Prior to this it was a Surgical Hospital

boys remained for two years. The four assistants or under-masters began, each in turn, with a first year class of rudimentary Latin, and carried the same boys forward through the stages of second, third and fourth classes, till, at the close of the four years, their pupils entered the fifth class. The masters then began afresh with a new set of beginners.

Robert was enrolled at first in the class of George Irvine and then in the class of Dr Aglionby-Ross Carson, the Rector, who came from the same part of Dumfriesshire as Robert's father and had been educated at the same school. Later rectors were administrators rather than teachers, but not at this stage. An outstanding classical scholar, Carson turned down an invitation to be professor of Greek at the University of St Andrews in favour of the High School. He opened up to McCheyne the literature of Greece and Rome. The Rector had about 250 boys in his class, whom he taught using a monitorial

Left: Initials scratched by pupils on the wall by the entrance to the Old Royal High, shortly before Robert arrived there

system, instituted by one of his predecessors, James Pillans. It worked as follows: the boys were divided into groups of nine or ten. Each group or class had a monitor, who heard the rest recite what they were taught. In each room there was a custodian who carefully watched the boys' behaviour and administered necessary discipline. All the groups recited the same lesson at the same time, creating a great deal of noise. Besides Latin and Greek, lessons were given on English Grammar and Composition (both in prose and verse) and geography. Quicker pupils were encouraged to study quietly while slower boys received the teacher's greater attention. Soon more regard was given to higher arithmetic, algebra, geometry and practical mathematics but this was a little later. Robert's aptitude for poetry and composition was nurtured in these classes.

We get a window into the excellence of the standards reached in the school through a report by assessors to the Lord Provost on the fourth class in the school, that of Mr Gray, for the year ending August 1820. We do not know the purpose of the report, but it may be that Gray was a candidate for the headship of the school. The glowing report expresses surprise at the boys' attainments. One examiner wrote that he was 'never more gratified with my public examination.' Another wrote, 'No boys in any school would have stood on higher ground in their studies in the classics.' The report listed the boys as having read Sallust, Livy, Tacitus, Cicero and Tibullus in Latin, and Horace, extracts from the Septuagint (the Greek translation of the Old Testament), Aesop's Fables and Homer in Greek. In addition, some boys did more advanced private study in Latin and Greek.

Two years before Robert left the school, a memorable event took place in which he must have

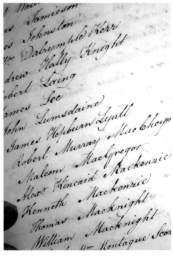

Above, left: Memorial to Aglionby-Ross Carson at the Royal Mile entrance of St Giles Cathedral
Above, right: The Day Book of the High School Library 1823–26, containing McCheyne's name

Above: The Royal High School, built between 1825–29, home to the school until the 1960s when it moved to the Barnton district of Edinburgh

shared. Bursting at the seams in Infirmary Street, the High School needed to move to larger premises. Several possible sites were considered and the Town Council decided to erect a new building on a bank of the Carlton Hill, an ideal location because of its centrality and accessibility to the old as well as the new town. Once the decision had been made, swift action followed. On 25 June 1825 Robert joined the other boys in a ceremonial march from Infirmary Street to Carlton Hill for the laying of the foundation stone by Lord Glenorchy; they were accompanied by the Rector and his colleagues, the Lord Provost, several magistrates, the university senate, office-bearers of the Grand Lodge, the sheriff and many other officials and leading citizens. Four years to the day, the school moved into its new home. Meanwhile McCheyne had left for university with particular merit in recitation and geography.

For McCheyne, a significant friendship began at school that lasted all his life. It was at the High School that he met Alexander Somerville. They sat together and were always in one another's company—like each other's shadow. A contemporary describes how if you saw one of them, it was not long before you saw the other. Their friendship matured at university and then in theological training, although at this stage it was not a spiritual or Christian friendship as it later became. Andrew Bonar was also a pupil in the school at the same time. Another of his school friends remembers the envy he felt at Robert's possession of a pair of tartan trousers! The same friend describes him as 'a tall slender lad with a sweet pleasant face, bright yet grave, fond of play, and of a blameless life.' Robert's education at the High School ended with the

Above: Caricature of Alexander Somerville,1875, one of McCheyne's best friends from childhood, an important figure in the Free Church of Scotland and its Moderator in 1886 (artist unknown)

session that began in March 1827.

McCheyne was not yet a Christian although he may have thought of himself as such. 'I knew not my danger, and felt not my load' was the way he later described his position. He had a considerable number of Christian connections. In these early years the family attended the Tron Church and he and other children remained behind to be instructed in the catechism and hymns.

Many Christian ministers visited the family home. Among them were his mother's brother Robert, his cousin William McCheyne, a near relative James Roddick, and a good friend James Grierson. Visits to Ruthwell meant times in the home of Henry Duncan, the parish minister. Like all children, he must have listened in on many interesting and helpful conversations. However, a sad death was to bring Robert to an awareness of his need of salvation.

Alexander Somerville (1813–1889)

Somerville was a friend of McCheyne in both his unconverted days and after his conversion; they studied theology together. They met for the study of the Bible using both the Greek translation of the Old Testament (the Septuagint) and the Hebrew original. More often they met to pray and share their Christian experience. Alexander began his ministry in a similar church extension charge to that of McCheyne in Anderston, Glasgow. Later in life his evangelistic zeal was renewed and fired by the ministry in Scotland of Moody and Sankey. At the surprising age of sixty-one he responded to God's call to be what may be described as an itinerant missionary travelling in India, Australasia, France, Italy, Germany, Russia, South Africa, Greece and Western Asia. He was Moderator of the Free Church General Assembly in 1886.

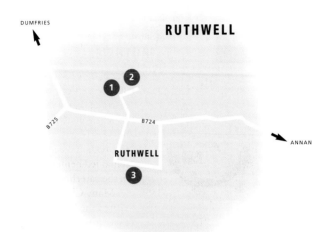

RUTHWELL

DUMFRIES

B725

B724

ANNAN

RUTHWELL

1 RUTHWELL CHURCH
2 THE OLD RUTHWELL MANSE, LATTERLY A HOTEL
3 THE SAVINGS BANK MUSEUM

TRAVEL INFORMATION

Ruthwell

Ruthwell is somewhat off the beaten track but both it and the surrounding area are well worth a visit. It is two and a half hours by car from Edinburgh and 45 minutes from Carlisle. From the A74 (M) take the A75 signposted South West Scotland, Dumfries, and Stranraer. Then turn left on to a road signposted Cummertrees, Ruthwell. Next turn right on to the B724, marked on our map. When you arrive at Ruthwell, a very narrow road on the right leads to the church and the road, directly opposite, goes into the village where the Savings Bank Museum is situated.
(www.savingsbankmuseum.co.uk).

Annan

Annan is twenty minutes away by car from Ruthwell and its parish church is where Edward Irving (See page 38) ministered and a statue of him is outside the church. It was here that McCheyne was licensed by the presbytery to preach the gospel as a probationer (see chapter 3 page 44) and where Henry Duncan presided over the church court that deposed Edward Irving from his ministry.

Edinburgh Travel

For details of daily train services to Edinburgh phone National Rail ☎ 08457 484950.
www.nationalrail.co.uk
For information on bus and coach services, phone Travel Line ☎ 0131 225 3858.
(www.travelline.co.uk).
For Edinburgh Airport ☎ 0131 333 1000.
(www.edinburghairport.com).

Edinburgh Tourist Information

Both www.visitscotland.com and www.edinburgh.org are worth visiting and they provide complementary information.

MAP SHOWING POSITION OF
RUTHWELL

A7

A76

DUMFRIES

A75

GRETNA

1

B721

SOLWAY FIRTH

CARLISLE

1 RUTHWELL

The three Edinburgh addresses of the McCheyne family—14 Dublin Street, 56 Queen Street and 20 Hill Street—are within easy walking distance of each other and are all behind Princes Street, on the side where all the shops are found. Infirmary Street, the site of the High School when McCheyne attended it, is on the opposite side of Princes Street, the Castle side.

St Giles' Cathedral

St Giles' is located on the Royal Mile in the heart of Edinburgh's Old

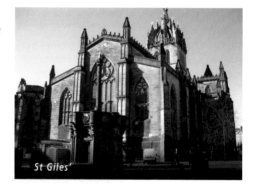

St Giles'

Town, close to Edinburgh Castle, the Museum of Scotland and the Palace of Holyrood House, a short walk from Waverley railway station. Buses 35, 23, 27, 28, 41 and 42 all pass close-by.

The Cathedral is the equivalent in Scotland of Westminster Abbey in England and is the principal church of Presbyterianism, the Church of Scotland. Special national

EDINBURGH

SEE ALSO MAPS ON PAGES 30 AND 45

celebrations take place within it, and the Chapel of the Order of the Thistle (Scotland's chivalric company of knights headed by the Queen) is there. A famous riot took place at the church in 1637 when the King in London sought to impose a new prayer book written by Archbishop Laud. The story goes that the riot started when an Edinburgh woman called Jenny Geddes threw her stool at the Dean. A sculpture of a stool in memory of her is in the Cathedral. In Parliament Square by the side of St Giles is where the Signet Library, important for McCheyne's father as a Writer to the Signet, is located.

(www.stgilescathedral.org.uk).

Below: Tempus Fugit (time flies) in Princes Street Gardens, an old clock made and maintained by James Ritchie

❷ Loss turned to gain

God did not figure in McCheyne's thinking as he began his student life. But the death of his brother David, a committed Christian, deeply affected him and brought about a profound change of direction

In 1827 at the age of fourteen, Robert entered Edinburgh University. While fourteen seems young to us, the pattern at the time for Scottish university students was to arrive in their early teens for a four year course. The transition from school to university was probably not difficult for Robert since the Old College, around which student activity centred, was literally a stone's throw from the High School in Infirmary Street; and the pattern of teaching to begin with was not dissimilar from that of the school.

First-year students joined 'junior' classes of Latin (known as humanity), Greek and Mathematics, each of which was taught at two levels. Logic and rhetoric (later renamed English literature) formed the next stage, and moral and natural philosophy (mathematically based physics) completed the tally of seven subjects. This was a common pattern across Europe. What we would call the study of the arts was a preparation for the study of medicine, law and theology. After two years of classical and mathematical study, students went on to a further two years of philosophy.

Above: The High School at the end of Infirmary Street

Facing page: The Old College of the University of Edinburgh where McCheyne studied from the age of fourteen

University Life

The University of Edinburgh was an exciting environment since it was at one of its numerical and developmental peaks and could boast of some exceptional teachers. It ranked among the largest universities in Europe. Classes tended to be huge, with between 130 to 200 students attending lectures in standard arts subjects. Most professors delivered lectures five days a week, but that was often the limit of their contact with students, although there were some outstanding exceptions. Lectures were not compulsory, and teachers tended to know little about their students. A few professors put questions to their classes and corrected written essays, but that was not the norm.

Written examinations were not introduced until the 1830s and 40s and so students were left much to themselves. If a student wanted to distinguish himself he could aim at accumulating class certificates and better still compete for class prizes. Once a course was completed, the class certificate was endorsed on the back. Formal graduation at the end of the four years was uncommon because it meant extra fees. Although the number of students was high, fewer than half a dozen students graduated each year.

In spite of the deficiencies of the system, Robert was blessed with some excellent teachers who no doubt inspired his thirst for knowledge. Two of McCheyne's professors made a profound impression upon him in these early years of study, perhaps because they were rather colourful

Above: Edinburgh University in South Bridge Street in the 19th century

Above: *Edinburgh University today—the McEwan Hall where graduations take place*

Facing page: Bust of *James Pillans, from the Cultural Collection, Edinburgh University Library*

Below: *John Wilson, whose pseudonym was Christopher North*

characters according to contemporary descriptions.

The first was James Pillans, the Professor of Humanity (Latin) and Laws, a born teacher and a former headmaster of the High School for ten years, having left the school the year before McCheyne joined it in 1821. He used to say that he was happy only when he was teaching. It was his success at the High School that led to his university appointment. Small in stature, he was eccentric in his taste in clothes. For important occasions he wore a white beaver hat and put on a blue coat with brass buttons. Refusing to wear spectacles, he used an enormous magnifying glass to read his lecture notes. Having introduced the monitorial system of teaching in the High School, he adopted the same system for his university classes, only this time calling the monitors, 'inspectors'. He had the distinction of inventing the blackboard and the coloured chalks that he used to teach geography. We take for granted

Sir Walter Scott (1771–1832)

Like McCheyne, Walter Scott was born in Edinburgh and his father was also a Writer to the Signet. Scott's attendance at the High School began forty-two years before that of McCheyne. He created historical novels and made them popular, especially in a series called the Waverley Novels. In the year McCheyne entered university, Scott published his *Life of Napoleon* in nine volumes. Scott was then at the peak of his

productivity and celebrity status, and he provides insight into the prevailing influences of the time. Like many others of his day, he was affected by what is known as the 18th century enlightenment that believed human reason could be used to combat ignorance, superstition,

and tyranny, and that it could build a better world. One of its principal targets was religion, particularly the Catholic Church in France. David Hume, the influential Scottish philosopher, was part of this movement and his writings were marked by scepticism and atheism. Hume criticized the standard proofs for God's existence, traditional ideas of God's nature and authority, the connection between morality and religion, and the reasonableness of belief in miracles. Scott was born five years before Hume died.

Above: Sir Walter Scott Monument in Princes Street

laptop computers and PowerPoint presentations, internet access and overhead projectors but the invention of the blackboard or chalkboard was equally revolutionary and innovative. Robert's increased grasp of Latin stood him in good stead and he often used it in his diary.

The second influential teacher was John Wilson, also known by his pen name Christopher North. His appointment in 1823 to the important and prestigious post of Professor of Moral Philosophy was controversial, basically because he was said to know little about the subject, something he freely admitted. Born in Scotland,

he had been educated at Glasgow University and Magdalen College, Oxford, where he graduated with distinction. Originally of independent means, his appointment in Edinburgh was a political one on account of his Tory sympathies, and was backed by Sir Walter Scott, one of his friends. His principal attainments were as a writer and journalist. What he lacked in his ability to teach moral philosophy was compensated for in the eyes of many of his students by his attractive character. He would have been described today as 'flashy'. He captured their respect by his reputation for

Left: *Statue of David Hume in the Royal Mile, Edinburgh—the rationalist and opponent of biblical authority who died in 1776, but whose influence was still felt at the time McCheyne was at university*

Right: *McCheyne's home at 56 Queen Street during the time he was at university*

flamboyancy, his wit, eloquence, and rather shocking manner of dress. His broad-brimmed hat could be instantly recognised. Beneath it his dishevelled sandy-coloured hair was like an unkempt mane that fell over his shoulders. His clothes were often threadbare, and his shirts button-less. Three or four Scotch terriers regularly scampered at his heels and were permitted to follow him into the classroom and crouch under his desk.

As a class began, Wilson had a habit of marching up to the desk and flinging on to it a collection of grubby envelopes upon which were written his lecture notes. Nevertheless he had an ability to stimulate his hearers' thought, although on reflection perceptive students recognised that his speeches were not as brilliant as they sounded at the time.

Whenever he entered a classroom he was greeted with applause and at the least opportunity he was cheered at comments he made in his lectures. John Wilson was a character and a half!

Thomas Carlisle's conviction was that more than anyone else he had ever seen, Wilson had the makings of a great man but that the great man never could be made. His students testified to his being much more accessible than most other teachers and one who proved a good counsellor and friend. His home was always open to them.

Other professors were not such memorable characters but equally able teachers who stimulated McCheyne's interest in Greek, science, mathematics and logic.

George Dunbar, Professor of Greek, wrote Greek grammars, histories and lexicons and encouraged McCheyne's interest in Greek customs and arts. William Wallace, Professor of Mathematics, was the inventor of instruments for transcribing mathematical figures and contributed to the Encyclopaedia Britannica. David Ritchie, Professor of Logic, and also minister of St Andrew's Church in Edinburgh, gave McCheyne a taste for philosophy. All the subjects he studied fed his mind and broadened his horizons. Later they provided a rich source of illustrations in his preaching.

A diligent student—who might have done better!

If students were not self-motivated, the danger of underachievement and mental stagnation was real. Helpful competition and a sense of achievement were generally lacking. In God's providence, McCheyne seems to have risen above these temptations to slackness. He took notes in the lectures he attended, reviewed them in the evening and rewrote them. Years later he advised a young student: 'If you acquire slovenly or sleepy habits of study now, you will never get the better of it.' He found pleasure and relaxation in composing poetry and enjoying music. In private he studied modern languages and engaged in gymnastics. Robert's home background and the encouragement of parents and siblings seem to have proved sufficient to deliver him from mediocrity.

In the light of the deficiencies of the system of education in the university, it is the more significant that McCheyne gained prizes in all the various classes that he attended. In John Wilson's class for example, he was awarded the prize for the best composition, a twenty-page poem on 'The Covenanters'. At the end of his course he received praise for being 'a distinguished student'.

McCheyne's father, however, thought that he could have done better! He wrote, 'Robert, though perfectly correct in his conduct, was of a more lively turn than David, and during the first three years of his attendance at University turned his attentions to elocution and poetry and the pleasures of society rather more,

Above: *St Stephen's Church, Edinburgh, attended by the McCheyne family from 1829*

perhaps, than was wise. His powers of singing and reciting were at that time very great and his company was courted on that account more than was favourable to graver pursuits.'

University provided opportunity for an active social life of parties and dances. In his own words, 'he kissed the rose nor thought about the thorn' and his 'song and laugh were loudest of the loud'. There were several young ladies to whom he sent valentines and for whom he composed poetry!

The McCheyne family moved around the churches of Edinburgh over the years. In 1829 they went as a family to St Stephen's Church, attracted perhaps by its reasonable proximity and newness. A massive structure in the Stockbridge district of Edinburgh's New Town, its sloping site was a challenge to William Playfair in 1828. The minister was William Muir, a man of evangelical sympathies but not a committed evangelical.

A great loss and turning point

Robert was much closer to his brother David than to William, and when David died suddenly on 8 July 1831, shortly after William had left for India to work with the Bengal Medical Service, it forced Robert to think seriously about his need of salvation. David was a committed Christian who prayed regularly for Robert and often spoke to him about the Christian life and his need of a personal relationship to God. At David's death, Robert tried to draw a portrait from memory of his brother but gave up the attempt and resorted instead to poetry in which he wrote of his brother's concern for him:

'Ah! how oft that eye would turn on me,
  with pity's tenderest look,
  and, only half-upbraiding, bid me flee
  from the vain idols of my boyish heart!'

In another poem about the same time he wrote,

'I sometimes … see him stand beside my bed … and bid me rest nor night nor day till I can say that

Above: The Revd William Muir in 1841

I have found the holy ground in which there lies the Pearl of Price.'

David had expressed the hope that Robert might one day become a minister of the gospel.

David had good reason for concern about Robert, since his behaviour was that of a talented and self-confident adolescent teenager caught up in the whirl of student social life and activity. Parties and dances and competing for the admiration of his female friends were important to him. The Roman and Greek classics in which he revelled influenced him more than the Bible and Christian teaching. Robert later expressed the thought that it was important for students to know the classics 'only as chemists handle poisons—to discover their qualities, not to infect their blood with them.'

Faith in Christ

David's prayers for his brother received their answer through his own premature death at the age of twenty-six. It had a profound effect upon Robert for his spiritual good. He knew in his heart that he did not have the genuine experience of the Lord Jesus Christ that his brother had so clearly possessed, and it prompted him to read the *Sum of Saving Knowledge* in the *Westminster Confession of Faith*. He later testified that this was, 'The work

---

David McCheyne (1804–1831)

As the eldest brother, it was perhaps natural for David to take up law as his career—the same profession as his father—and he worked with him as an apprentice for five years, and then remained with him as an associate after his admittance to the Society of the Signet in 1826. The circumstances of his conversion are not known but during the last years of his life his mind became deeply impressed with eternal realities, and his father spoke of him being of 'the greatest use to his two younger brothers … teaching them down to the day of his death'. Robert never spoke of David without referring to his spiritual influence. In a letter to a boy in August 1836 he wrote, 'I had a kind brother as you have, who taught me many things. He gave me a Bible, and persuaded me to read it; he tried to train me as a gardener trains the apple-tree upon the wall; but all in vain. I thought myself wiser than he, and would always take my own way; and many a time, I well remember, I have seen him reading his Bible, or shutting his closet door to pray, when I have been dressing to go to some frolic, or some dance of folly.' In 1842 he wrote to Andrew Bonar, 'This day eleven years ago I lost my loved and loving brother, and began to seek a Brother who cannot die.'

Above: David McCheyne from a miniature. No date is given

Left: The Signet Library in the shadow of St Giles, Edinburgh. The Signet Society is a private society of Scottish solicitors whose history goes back to the 14th century

which I think first of all wrought a saving change in me. How gladly would I renew the reading of it if that change might be carried on to perfection.' Conviction of sin slowly dawned upon him. He saw his original sin not as an excuse for his sins, but as an aggravation of them. He became aware of his guilt before God in a way he had not known before. Previously he would have acknowledged it if pressed, but his awareness of it did not bring about a change of heart. Now it did! Without fail at every anniversary of his brother's death he recalled his influence upon him. His father confirmed this: 'The holy example and the happy death of his brother David seems by the blessing of God to have given a new impulse to his mind in the right direction.'

Robert's conversion showed itself in the change in his life. On the inside cover of a notebook containing his somewhat pretentious and affected essays and poems, he expressed his shame at what he had written and his awareness that lighter pursuits like playing cards and dancing had to go. He began to share in the work of the church's Sunday school. No doubt influenced by his brother's conviction that the ministry is 'the most blessed work on earth', and as a result of his brother's prayers, Robert presented himself to the Edinburgh Presbytery of the Church of Scotland as a candidate for the ministry. On the 28 September 1831 he was examined by them and allowed to proceed. His studies now had a new and better motivation and focus.

SEE ALSO MAPS ON PAGES 19 AND 45

ST.STEPHEN
STREET

② HOWE STREET

EDINBURGH

QUEEN STREET

GEORGE STREET

PRINCES STREET

LEITH STREET

NORTH BRIDGE

① LOTHIAN RD

HIGH STREET

SOUTH BRIDGE

CHAMBERS STREET

③

④ INFIRMARY STREET

1   ST CUTHBERT'S CHURCH
2   ST STEPHEN'S CHURCH, STOCKBRIDGE
3   THE OLD COLLEGE, EDINBURGH UNIVERSITY
4   INFIRMARY STREET AND THE OLD HIGH SCHOOL BUILDING

TRAVEL INFORMATION

For Edinburgh Travel Information see Chapter One (page 17).

St Cuthbert's Parish Church, Edinburgh

Edinburgh, EH1 2EP. ☎ 0131 229 1142

Located at the west end of Princes Street Gardens, on the corner of Lothian Road and King's Stables Road. There are entrances into the churchyard from Princes Street, West Princes Street Gardens, Kings Stables Road and Lothian Road. In the grounds of the graveyard McCheyne's parents are

Above: St Cuthbert's Church, Edinburgh

Above: McCheyne family grave in St Cuthbert's Graveyard

buried, and there is a stone memorial to the whole family. If your visit is in the summer, the church café holds a register and plan of the graves that is helpful for visitors.

The Old College, Edinburgh University

This building is the work of two famous architects: Robert Adam and William Playfair. Its foundation stone was laid in 1789. The original plan for the building was Robert Adam's, and he died in 1792. The Napoleonic Wars hindered work, and William Playfair was appointed to complete the building in 1816 when he was only twenty-seven. McCheyne and his contemporaries must have been aware of the newness of the building since it was completed only in the 1820s. The present dome, intended from the beginning of the plans, was not put in place until the University's 300th anniversary in 1883. (www.ed.ac.uk/buildings/oldcollege.html).

St Stephen's Church, Stockbridge

The church is best approached down Howe Street and St Vincent Street and it is well worth seeing. The exterior is basically square but diagonally-built with a corner facing the street, to which an arched porch entrance is attached. Underneath the church are tunnel-vaulted cellars. They once housed an evening school, the brainchild of William Muir, the first minister, so that illiterate members of his parish could receive education.

Below: Edinburgh University Quadrangle in McCheyne's time

Bottom: The Old College Dome, Edinburgh

❸ A new sense of direction

McCheyne's experience of new birth brought a sense of
vocation that he had not before known. This expressed itself
in his entering the Divinity Hall of Edinburgh University.
Godly theological teachers and stimulating Christian
fellowship with other students fostered his spiritual growth

Two and a half months after
his brother David's death,
Robert presented himself to
the Edinburgh Presbytery of the
Church of Scotland as a candidate
to study Divinity at the University.
This was the required pattern, and
all university professors in theology
were ministers of the Church of
Scotland. He began his studies in
the winter of 1831.

While spiritual change is
immediate upon new birth, the
changes do not all take place at
once. However, some were soon
noticeable in Robert's attitudes.
During his first years at university
studying the arts, he had not been
engrossed in his studies, even
though he did well in them. With
his study of theology it was quite
different: he was soon to find
himself totally absorbed—but that
was not immediately the case.

When Robert began his divinity
course it did not require much to
encourage him to spend his time in
light-hearted and trivial leisure
activities. His diary reveals how this
altered during the first two years.
Less than six months after the
beginning of his course we find him
writing in his diary: 'I hope never to
play cards again.' The following
month, he recorded, 'Absented

*Above: The Old College where the
Divinity Hall was housed in
McCheyne's time*

*Facing page: John Knox statue in the
courtyard of New College, Edinburgh.
Many papers concerning McCheyne
are kept in the college library*

Chalmers first came to public attention as a preacher when he was minister of the Tron Church in Glasgow (not the well-known Tron Church in today's city centre), and then St John's Church—Renfield in Kelvindale. At the age of forty-eight he went to Edinburgh, and his lectures were immediately popular and packed not only with theological students but with distinguished members of the Edinburgh community. People were attracted by his teaching ability and depth of learning. A key benefit of Chalmers' influence upon his students was that he was always aware that they were prospective pastors and teachers. His lectures in practical and pastoral theology were formative for them and he gave rise, in God's providence, to an active and earnest generation of pastors, among whom were McCheyne and his friends.

Above:
Thomas Chalmers.

myself from the dance.' His attitude to life became more adult and sensible, as he became aware of his inner corruption and weakness and his need to depend wholly on the finished work of the Lord Jesus Christ. His diary record coincides with his genuine Christian experience. He wrote in it what was, in effect, a confession and prayer to God: 'Leaning on a staff of my own devising, it betrayed me, and broke under me. It was not Thy staff. Resolving to be a god, Thou showedst me that I was but a man. But my own staff being broken, why may I not lay hold of Thine?' With that acknowledgement came an appreciation of the Cross. A month later he wrote, 'Have found much rest in Him who bore all our burdens for us.' Robert began to get up early each morning to seek God, commenting, 'Who would not rise early to meet much company?'

Mentors for the ministry

Discussion regularly surrounds the best way to train and equip men to be pastors and teachers. Each generation tends to vary the pattern. Without entering into that debate certain undeniably important parts are identifiable such as excellent theological teaching, stimulating spiritual fellowship with one's peers, preachers who provide good role models, and hands-on experience of Christian service. These provide a helpful basis for exploring what made McCheyne's years in Divinity Hall so profitable.

McCheyne sat in the classes of three professors who had a profound influence upon him and his contemporaries. The 'icing on the cake' was Thomas Chalmers, the outstanding member of the Divinity Faculty. His teaching was all the more telling and significant

Right: The Revd.John Hunter (left) and Professor Alexander Brunton (right), 1839, ministerial colleagues at the Tron Church, Edinburgh

Below: Alexander Brunton was McCheyne's Professor of Hebrew in the Divinity Hall at Edinburgh University

because he had not always been an evangelical. He was not only a theological lecturer but also an excellent preacher.

The second important teacher was the Professor of Hebrew, Alexander Brunton. An expert in oriental languages, he taught his students not only grammar and vocabulary but also the life and customs of the East. He was at the same time minister of the Tron Church in Edinburgh. Although McCheyne would not have been drawn to him theologically or spiritually in the same way as he would to the other professors, he was fascinated by his lectures and his painstaking exegesis of the books of the Old Testament.

The third lecturer was the Professor of History, David Welsh, who began his teaching the year McCheyne commenced his theological studies. He was the least eminent of the three professors in the Divinity Hall, not because of the importance of his subject, but simply because at the time there was little interest in Scotland in the history of the church outside of Scotland. Unlike his colleagues, Welsh did not combine university work with a church appointment or preaching. He influenced his students not only by his lectures but by his personal spiritual devotion to Christ, and his obvious care and concern for them shone out. The question he asked himself about every student was: 'How can I do him good?' We are able to listen in, as it were, to his lectures because in 1844 he decided to publish them. The first book begins: 'The object of Church History is to give an account of the rise and progress, the vicissitudes and characters of that spiritual kingdom, which the Almighty has established on earth under the administration of his Son Jesus Christ.' There can be little doubt that these were his first words to his students in church history.

Not by human design but clearly by God's gracious providence, McCheyne had the best of teachers. At the same time he became aware of the dangers of theological study, especially through the benefit he gained from reading the works of Jonathan Edwards. Robert entered into his diary: 'Oh that heart and understanding may grow together, like brother and sister, leaning on one another!' At the same time he developed high views of pastoral ministry. At the end of his first year he wrote, 'How apt are we to lose our hours in the vainest babblings, as do the world! How can this be with those chosen for the mighty office? fellow-workers with God? heralds of His Son? evangelists? men set apart to the work, chosen out of the chosen … who are to shine as the stars for ever and ever?' A year later he discovered great enjoyment in preparing sermons, which he called 'a pleasant kind of labour'. But he also appreciated its dangers: 'I fear the love of applause or effect goes a long way. May God keep me from preaching myself instead of Christ crucified.'

His friends in training

McCheyne's spiritual relationship with fellow divinity students was also significant. As we have seen earlier, he already had a good friendship with Alexander Somerville, and both were converted at around the same time. They were soon sharing times of Bible study and prayer, and it was a case of iron sharpening iron as they

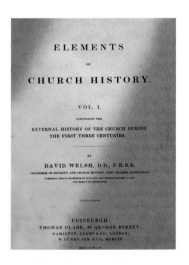

Above: Frontispiece of David Welsh's book 'Elements of Church History'

Top, centre: David Welsh

Above: Arthur's Seat, Edinburgh, where McCheyne often walked in deep discussion with his college friends

Below, top: Alexander Somerville

Below, bottom: Horatius Bonar, one of McCheyne's close friends at Divinity college

encouraged and built one another up in their Christian discipleship.

In the first year at Divinity Hall both McCheyne and Somerville became friends with the two brothers, Horatius and Andrew Bonar. Duddingston Loch and Arthur's Seat in Edinburgh, as well as the lochs and hills around Edinburgh, were places they delighted to walk together, discussing, as theological students do, the issues of the day and their hopes for their future ministries. During the summer breaks they agreed to continue meeting for theological study and reading the Bible in Hebrew and Greek. Andrew Bonar prompted their discussion on theories about the millennium. While interested in them, McCheyne did not commit himself to adopting any particular viewpoint. If the test of friendship is time, then these friendships proved their enduring value.

Preaching role models

As important as theological professors in the training of pastors and teachers is the role-model of preachers under whom they are able to sit week by week. McCheyne's parents and family seem to have moved around the churches, no doubt because of the benefit they gained from the preaching of their pastors. William Muir, minister of St Stephen's Church, the family's

Edward Irving (1792–1834)

Irving was both a colourful and controversial character. He was born in Annan, Dumfriesshire, where a statue of him stands outside the Old Parish Church. Licensed to preach in 1815, he became Thomas Chalmers' assistant at St John's in Glasgow in 1819. In 1822, having become minister of London's Scottish congregation in Hatton Garden, he became something of a sensation as the initial congregation of fifty or so grew so that they moved to a new church in Regent Square in 1827. He sadly became involved in controversy over the humanity of Christ and he welcomed the manifestation of speaking in tongues—though he himself never spoke in tongues—prophecies and miraculous healing in the church, bitterly dividing the church. His elders opposed him and the trustees of Regent Square banned him from the building in 1832 and the Church of Scotland deposed him from its ministry in 1833. The consequence was the establishment by his followers of a new sect that became known as the Irvingites.

Somerville where John Bruce was minister. McCheyne's sister said that 'he regarded Mr Bruce with warmest love and reverence, prizing every word that fell from his lips.' We know from his diary that he took copious notes of Bruce's sermons and then wrote them up on a Sunday evening. Bruce's style as a preacher was complicated and he was somewhat extravagant in his gestures and mannerisms. What was especially striking was his boldness and authority.

The third preacher was Alexander Moody (pictured left)—known later as Moody Stuart after his marriage to Jessie Stuart. He was only four years older than McCheyne. When McCheyne heard him he is recorded as saying, 'I have found the man.' Moody had a similar appreciation of Robert for he later wrote, 'It was to me a golden day when I first became acquainted with a young man so full of Christ.' McCheyne was responsible for introducing both Somerville and the Bonars to Moody, and they met in Moody's house each week for an hour of prayer. They formed the nucleus of what became known as 'the McCheyne group.'

Hands-on experience

Chalmers encouraged McCheyne to join the Missionary Association of the Divinity Hall. Its object was to stimulate its members to devote an hour or two each week visiting the spiritually

church at this time, was initially the man Robert heard most frequently. As a capital city, Edinburgh's churches had many visiting preachers, among whom was Edward Irving who unfailingly attracted huge crowds.

Three preachers are especially worthy of mention. Thomas Chalmers comes at the top of the list and he was at the height of his powers at this time. McCheyne sometimes went to the New North Parish Church with Alexander

Above: Duddingston Loch, another favourite haunt of McCheyne, the Bonar brothers and Alexander Somerville

careless and needy in the most neglected parts of central Edinburgh. This was not intended to distract them from study, but was to be taken out of time that would otherwise have been spent on recreation. The programme was to meet for prayer on a Saturday morning in Dr Chalmers' vestry and then to visit from door to door. Once more his friendship with Somerville comes to the fore, and they gave their time to the Canongate district, in the area around Riddle's Entry, where more than three hundred people lived in just forty-seven houses. They started a Sunday school and distributed what was called *The Monthly Visitor*.

McCheyne began this evangelistic work somewhat nervously: 'Visited two families with tolerable success. God grant a blessing may go with us! Began in fear and weakness, and in much trembling. May the power be of God.' Such work was an eye-opener for him, coming as he did from a privileged background, and it affected him greatly: 'Ah! why am I such a stranger to the poor of my native town? I have passed their door thousands of times. ... Why should I give hours and days any longer to the vain world, when there is such a world of misery at my very door?'

Like contemporary universities, there were other societies, and those special to theological students. One, called the Exegetical Society, formed again at the suggestion of Thomas Chalmers, was especially important for McCheyne. With only eighteen members–the best students in Greek and Hebrew–it met at six-thirty every Saturday morning and its primary concern was to study the Bible and its exegesis (understanding the text of the Bible). Chalmers suggested that 'none but the very elite of the Hall for taste and skill in the languages should be admitted to it.' Members took it in turns each week to read an essay and then to chair the meeting the following week. They recorded their proceedings and eventually bound them together. They signed a covenant on 24 May 1838 in these terms: 'We the undersigned members of the Exegetical Society hereby declare our intention to read during the course of next year the Books of Isaiah and Jeremiah or one or other of them in Hebrew—and one of the books of the New Testament in Greek.' McCheyne's was the final signature of the seven, and

Above: 'The Monthly Visitor' the evangelistic paper distributed by McCheyne and his friends in a poor district of Edinburgh

Above: The Canongate as it was in the 19th century

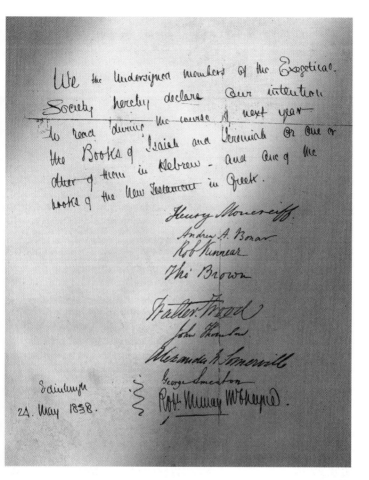

Above: The Covenant of the members of the Exegetical Society to study the Scriptures

included were those of Andrew Bonar and Alexander Somerville.

Three other factors at this impressionable time were of significance. The first was McCheyne's developing concern for foreign missions. The period was one when missionary biographies were popular and increasing, and articles relevant to the subject were often in print. Memorable was the return from India of Alexander Duff, the first Church of Scotland missionary there, and both McCheyne and Somerville spent time with him in the spring of 1835 when he was staying in Portobello, Edinburgh's seaside.

After his developing concern for foreign missions, the second factor was McCheyne's reading of significant books; they made an important impact upon him. He

Alexander Duff (1806–1878)

What Henry Martyn was to Anglicans and William Carey to Baptists, Duff was to Presbyterians. Born in Moulin, Perthshire, and educated at St Andrews University, he went to India in 1830. He established an English School in Calcutta, with a roll of 1,200 students. The teaching of the Bible was central. Scientific and other subjects were taught to university level. His example prompted similar work in Bombay and Madras. While back in Scotland on his first furlough he wrote *India and India Mission* and *Missions the Chief End of the Christian Church*—both in 1839. He was among those responsible for drawing up the constitution of Calcutta University and he helped launch the *Calcutta Review*. He also gave his support to those who sought to provide education for girls. After retiring from his work in India 1873, he became the Free Church Professor of evangelistic theology.

re-read *The Westminster Confession of Faith* and in particular the *Sum of Saving Knowledge* with which it begins. The latter is a brief summary of Christian doctrine. Along with this he read Thomas Adam's *Private Thoughts on Religion and other subjects* and the writings of Jonathan Edwards, the philosopher, theologian and preacher who had seen true spiritual revival in his church in New England, America during the 1740s.

Biographies had a special place in promoting Robert's spiritual growth. He read (in Latin) the life of Legh Richmond, an Anglican rector in Bedfordshire, who had been greatly influenced by William Wilberforce's *A Practical View of Christianity* and who wrote a 19th century Christian bestseller entitled *The Dairyman's Daughter* (See in this series *William Wilberforce—the friend of humanity* p 100.) As a result, McCheyne wrote, 'Never saw myself so vile, so useless, so poor, and, above all, so ungrateful.' Two missionary biographies deeply affected him, as they have done others throughout the generations. The first was the life of David Brainerd of whom he wrote, 'A most wonderful man! What conflicts, what depressions, desertions, strength, advancement, victories, within thy torn bosom! I cannot express what I think when I think of thee. To-night more set upon missionary enterprise than ever.' The next day he wrote, 'Oh for Brainerd's humility and self-loathing dispositions!' The second

Left: The Canongate Church on the Royal Mile, built in 1688, in whose parish is the Palace of Holyroodhouse, the Scottish Parliament, and Edinburgh Castle (even though the latter stands apart from the rest of the parish)

biography was the *Memoirs of Henry Martyn*: 'Would I could imitate him, giving up father, mother, country, house, health, life, all—for Christ. And yet, what hinders? Lord, purify me, and give me strength to dedicate myself, my all, to Thee!' McCheyne's deliberate purpose in reading these biographies was to discover and apply the principles of their godly lives to his own life.

The third significant factor influencing his life at this time was McCheyne's early exposure to church politics: politics not in the unfavourable use of the word but in terms of understanding how the church governed itself. Studying in Edinburgh gave opportunity to sit in on the meetings of the Presbytery and Synod. When the time came for the annual General Assembly he could listen to the debates and discussions.

Examined for the ministry

In terms of 19th century training for the ministry it is hard to think of a better environment and training. Half way through McCheyne's fourth year the time came for him to be examined before the Presbytery of Edinburgh for his license to preach. He wrote in his diary: 'Tomorrow I undergo my trials before Presbytery. May God give me courage in the hour of need. What should I fear? If God see meet to put me into the ministry, who shall keep me back? If I be not meet, why should I be thrust forward?' Part of the examination was the daunting prospect of preaching a trial sermon before his professors on 16 February 1835.

McCheyne's last day at college was 29 March 1835. But already interest was shown by a number of ministers in having him as their assistant. This led him—as was often done in such cases—to ask the Presbytery of Edinburgh, under whose superintendence he had carried on his studies, to transfer the remainder of his public trials to another Presbytery, where there would be less pressure of business to cause delay. This request was readily granted and his connection with Dumfriesshire led him to the Presbytery of Annan, the district from which his mother came. Further probationary sermons had to be preached and he was required to submit five linguistic and homiletical assignments. His examination proved satisfactory, and having signed the Confession of Faith, he was licensed 'to preach the gospel of our Lord and Saviour Jesus Christ as a probationer for the holy ministry.' This meant that he could preach but not dispense the sacraments. He could now look for a call to a church and then ordination would take place.

After being licensed on 1 July 1835, McCheyne's first sermons were preached at Ruthwell the following Sunday. In the morning he spoke on 'The Pool of Bethesda'; and in the afternoon on 'The Strait Gate'. He wrote in his diary: 'Found it a more awfully solemn thing than I had imagined, to announce Christ authoritatively; yet a glorious privilege!'

Above: Ruthwell Church where McCheyne preached his first sermon as a probationer minister on 1 July 1835

EDINBURGH

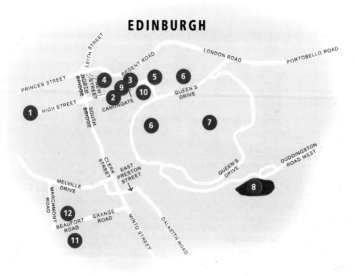

SEE ALSO MAPS ON PAGES 19 AND 30

1	EDINBURGH CASTLE	8	DUDDINGSTON LOCH
2	CANONGATE	9	THE PEOPLE'S STORY
3	CANONGATE CHURCH	10	THE SCOTTISH PARLIAMENT
4	NEW STREET	11	THE GRANGE CEMETERY
5	THE PALACE OF HOLYROOD	12	ST CATHERINE'S ARGYLE CHURCH
6	HOLYROOD PARK		
7	ARTHUR'S SEAT		

TRAVEL INFORMATION

Edinburgh Castle

The Castle is at the top of the Royal Mile and Holyrood Abbey at the bottom. The Castle is the most visited of Edinburgh's landmarks and each year hosts the world renowned Edinburgh Military Tattoo. Besides a place of defence for the city since 1085 it has also served in the past as a prison. (www.royalmile.com).

Canongate

This is at the Holyrood Abbey end of the Mile and it takes its name from the canons that once ran the abbey at Holyrood, and it was an independent burgh from Edinburgh from 1128 to 1636. 'Gate' in Scots means 'way' or 'street'.

Canongate church

Built in the 1680s, the churchyard contains the graves of some famous people. Of particular interest is the memorial to Horatius Bonar, one of McCheyne's friends and the writer of many hymns, including 'I heard the voice of Jesus say'.

The Palace of Holyroodhouse

Established as a monastery in 1128, the Palace of Holyroodhouse is the official Scottish residence of the Royal Family. It is used for state ceremonies and its gardens for royal garden parties. When the sovereign is not in residence, it is open to visitors. Details are found at www.royal.gov.uk

Above: The entrance to the Gardens of the Palace of Holyroodhouse

Holyrood Park

Known also as Queen's Park, because it is owned by the sovereign, it is nearly always open for the public. Entirely surrounded by the city of Edinburgh, its principal feature is Arthur's Seat, the main peak of a group of hills which form most of the Park. It provides some of the best views of the city and it is not difficult to climb.

Duddingston Loch

This attractive lake is a bird sanctuary and is noted for heron and great crested grebe and wintering wildfowl. Sir Henry Raeburn's famous picture of the Revd. Robert Walker skating (the minister of the Canongate church) has Duddingston Loch as its location. (www.natgalscot.ac.uk).

The People's Story

This free museum on the Royal Mile gives helpful insight into the life of ordinary people in Edinburgh from the 18th century onwards. It uses oral history, reminiscence, and written sources to tell their story. Disabled access to the first floor by lift. (www.cac.org.uk).

Above: The People's Story. A museum of the life of ordinary people in Edinburgh from the eighteenth century

Riddle's Entry

This no longer exists. It was in the Canongate area on the west side of New Street, where number 35 used to be. It probably owes its name to James Riddell, who was a smith or metal-worker in New Street. There is now nothing of interest to see, but in the mid 19th century it was so densely and unhealthily populated that its redevelopment was inevitable.

The Scottish Parliament

Scotland's Parliament sits at the foot of the Royal Mile directly opposite the Palace of Holyroodhouse. It is open to visitors and provides a restaurant. It has been the official home of the Scottish Parliament since September 2004. (www.scottish.parliament. uk).

Grange cemetery

Close to the Meadows in Edinburgh, the cemetery was opened in 1847 when it was then on the edge of the city. You do not have to wander far in it without finding many famous names in Christian history. The first Moderator of the Free Church of Scotland, Thomas Chalmers (1780–1847), Thomas Guthrie (1803–1873) and Alexander Duff (1806–1878) are buried here. Directly opposite the main entrance to the cemetery is St Catherine's Argyle Parish Church where Horatius Bonar was the first minister, although then called Chalmers Memorial Free Church. (http://www.stcatherines-argyle.org.uk/history).

Top: St Catherine's Argyle Church

Above: The Grave of Alexander Duff in the Grange Cemetery, Edinburgh. He was the first missionary of the Church of Scotland sent to India in 1829

The Scottish Parliament

❹ An eager apprentice

If Robert Murray McCheyne's university course prepared him academically, and his college course prepared him spiritually, it was his assistantship which provided him with the role model he required for pastoral work and the opportunity to establish habits and patterns of personal discipline that were to shape his future ministry

The interest shown in McCheyne led to an invitation to become assistant to the parish minister of Larbert in Stirlingshire. While waiting for it to be confirmed, he preached in various places, finding a ready acceptance of his teaching and preaching. He began work at Larbert on 7 November 1835. Robert was probably among the first of his contemporaries, if not the first, to be settled in an appointment. He and his family must have been particularly pleased because of its proximity to Edinburgh since Larbert is less than thirty miles (48.3 km) away and access had been made easier by the recent construction of the Union Canal.

The reputation of John Bonar, the parish minister, made the appointment additionally attractive. Twelve years older than McCheyne, he had a name for being among the best instructors and trainers of young assistants. McCheyne was to call him 'my good bishop'. Bonar was the

Above: The Union Canal from the Edinburgh end

Left, below: John Bonar under whom McCheyne served as an assistant

Facing page: Larbert Old Parish Church from its graveyard. It was in this church that McCheyne served as Bonar's assistant in 1835

parish minister from 1826 to 1843, when at the Disruption (described in Chapter 8) he became part of the Free Church. His example in pastoral visitation influenced him tremendously, and McCheyne learnt much from the way in which he instructed children and captured their interest and attention.

Larbert in the mid 19th century was only a large village. The Roman road from Falkirk to Stirling crossed the parish and evidences of it remain. The important river Carron was five

The Industrial Revolution

The application of power-driven machinery to manufacturing, turned Britain from a largely rural population dependent upon agriculture into a town-centred society with a focus upon industries based upon factories. Its primary development was in England from 1750 onwards, gradually gaining momentum throughout Britain up until 1830. Scotland's iron ore and coal deposits were exploited due to new inventions. What is particularly interesting is that the area in which McCheyne first worked, once an agricultural district, had become a thriving industrial centre due to the construction in 1759 of the Carron ironworks that marked the commencement of the Industrial Revolution in Scotland; it became the largest industrial plant in Scotland, smelting over 8000 tons of pig iron each year and boasting among its finished products the *carronades* used by the fighting ships and soldiers of Nelson and Wellington. The *carronade* was a short smoothbore, cast iron cannon, similar to a mortar, developed for the Royal Navy. HMS Victory used two 68-pounder *carronades* to great effect at the Battle of Trafalgar.

If you look at the back of many of the familiar red British pillar-boxes you will find that they contain the name of their maker, Carron. The iron works closed only in 1985.

Below, left: *A carronade*

Below, right: *A small post-box made by Carron*

Above: Painting of Larbert in McCheyne's time which hangs in the vestry of Larbert Old Parish Church

Below: A picture of McCheyne which also hangs in the vestry of Larbert Old Parish Church

miles (8 km) away, vital for the industry that was built upon its shores.

In 1790 Larbert was a community of 400 inhabitants, this increased to 4000 plus in 1831 and 6000 in 1835. The Industrial Revolution brought prosperity and with it spiritual indifference. The increasing population underlined Bonar's need for an assistant. The church in Larbert had been rebuilt in 1820 to cope with the increasing population and the new building with seating for 1200 was only fifteen years old when Robert arrived.

However, Larbert was not the extent of Bonar's responsibilities. He was also minister of nearby Dunipace, less than three miles (5 km) away, a place totally different from Larbert and much more attractive. Whereas Larbert was industrial, noisy and tended to be dirty, Dunipace was rural, quiet and free from heavy industry, much more like McCheyne's favourite area of Ruthwell in Dumfriesshire. Farmers and farm workers rather than coal-miners and iron-moulders formed the congregation. Here again the church building was recent. The old church, on a different site, had been replaced only the previous year by a new building, able to seat 604 people. The new church building prompted increased attendance. Again the population was growing. In 1831 it was 1,278 but in 1841 it had increased to 1,578.

The differences and complexities of the two church situations were an ideal opportunity for a young minister to learn to adapt to different extremes. The economic prosperity of the iron-smelting industry brought the acute problem of drunkenness to Larbert, a difficulty McCheyne was to meet later in Dundee. While only a relatively short distance separated the two parishes, their dissimilarity was immense. Besides these two churches, five other preaching stations in the parish increased the opportunity for regular preaching. McCheyne soon became impressed by the great opportunity, but overwhelmed by the impossibility of just two men coping with it. At the same time, working among the rough men of the ironworks he became acutely aware of his youthfulness and how inexperienced in life he must have

appeared to them—a not unfamiliar experience for young ministers and apprentices.

Health warning signs

Tiredness—physical, spiritual and emotional—is understandable when beginning pastoral responsibilities. It is not uncommon for preachers to be exhausted after a busy Sunday. But the endeavour to give equal attention to both parishes and to match the challenge of the numbers of people to visit, soon took their toll, accentuated by McCheyne's inherent physical weakness. He wrestled with exhaustion. Although he had only begun in early November, by the end of the year his heart was giving some concern because of its unpleasant and irregular beating and an irritating cough was bothering him. To his bitter disappointment he was instructed to take a month off, because his right lung was damaged and the air vessels clogged and irritated. His initial fear was that someone might have to replace him. He was grateful to be able to return to

Left: Minute Books of Larbert and Dunipace elders' meetings during McCheyne's time

Above: Dunipace church. John Bonar shared his ministry between Dunipace and Larbert, and McCheyne often preached here

Larbert but was aware that he could not be as active as he had hoped to be, and his ministry needed to be more in prayer and intercession than before.

As he became increasing sensitive to his physical limitations, McCheyne began to recognise God's fatherly discipline in them. Times of illness prompted him to examine his heart and confess, 'The lust of praise has ever been my besetting sin; and what more befitting school could be found for me than that of suffering alone, away from the eye and ear of man?'

Young people

John Bonar encouraged McCheyne in his desire to start instruction classes for the Larbert young people. They proved successful. Meeting in the tower of the church, up a narrow winding staircase, it is easy to imagine how

the young people must have enjoyed the sense of being apart from the adults and together. About sixty, with boys usually outnumbering girls, packed into the tower. His purpose was to 'try to entice them on—to know and love the Lord Jesus'. His aim was to 'entertain them to the utmost, and at the same time to win their souls'. At every opportunity he gathered ideas and object lessons to illustrate his teaching of the catechism.

Preaching

Larbert and Dunipace proved formative in McCheyne's development as a preacher. While John Bonar was his mentor, McCheyne did not follow him unthinkingly. Sensitive to the character of the congregations, he felt that John Bonar's hour and a half sermons were too long and he chose to aim at less than thirty-five minutes. The services at Larbert and Dunipace, together with the five preaching stations, gave ample opportunity for preaching, and on average McCheyne preached three times each Sunday, plus Bible classes and special meetings throughout the week. In preparation he was both careful and prayerful. He felt he could not feed others unless he had first fed himself on what he was going to share with them and what had cost him something in preparation.

His hearers found him practical and pointed. One, a Major Dundas of Carron Hall, listened to him preach on the parable of the sower and congratulated him 'on being the only minister I have heard tell the people their faults.' But McCheyne, like many a young preacher, became mindful of how careful he needed to be in handling rebuke in preaching. He found himself mourning his 'bitter speaking of the gospel. Surely it is a gentle message, and should be spoken with angelic tenderness, especially by such a needy sinner.' Significantly, when a friend mentioned speaking on the text that 'The wicked shall be turned into hell', McCheyne asked, 'Were you able to do it with tenderness?'

McCheyne's diary contains frequent references to his

Above: Both old and contemporary views of Old Parish House, Larbert

Left: The tower of Larbert Old Parish Church where McCheyne met with his group of young people

preaching, showing how concerned he was to improve his effectiveness. Without spelling out the mistake he had in mind, he wrote in March, 'Preached in Larbert with very much comfort, owing chiefly to my remedying the error of 21st February.' His comments show too how conscious he was of the need to die to himself in his preaching so that his motive was not his praise but God's. He wrote, 'How happy and strange is the feeling when God gives the soul composure to stand and plead for Him! Oh, that it were altogether for Him I plead, not for myself!' These moments of the discovery of his pride were both necessary and effective for they caused him to pray, 'Oh that these may keep me humble and be my burden, leading me to the cross. Then, Satan, thou wilt be outwitted!'

A small but significant incident influenced his style of preaching—the result of a preacher's nightmare. From the beginning he wrote out his sermons carefully, although determined neither to read nor recite them. His aim was to impress his notes on his memory and then to speak with the liberty given to him. But his notes were always there to reassure him and to aid his memory. One morning he had cause to ride to Dunipace quickly and without realising it dropped his notes on the way. When he arrived he was not able to refresh his memory as usual. To his surprise he was able to preach with greater freedom than before. He discovered that he had the gift of extemporary preaching and that he was more at ease than he would ever have imagined. He did not lay it down as a principle for

Robert Bruce 1554–1631

Left: *Robert Bruce, a leader in the Reformation in Scotland and the Laird of Kinnairds*

Below: *The grave of Robert Bruce*

An influential Reformation leader, Bruce was buried in the Larbert churchyard. His family claimed descent from King Robert the Bruce. He studied theology in St Andrews and was ordained in 1587 to become a minister at St Giles in Edinburgh. In 1596 he, with others, was banished from the city because he opposed James VI's determination to impose episcopacy on Scotland. During his banishment, he became the unpaid minister of Larbert parish. Allowed to return to Edinburgh, he was ordered away again in 1601 and for the last thirty years of his life

had no settled home. His preaching attracted great crowds and what he preached was matched by the life he lived. One of his disciples, John Livingstone, declared, 'No man since the apostles' time spake with such power.'

others but it was an important lesson for him. The experience was not a discovery of his own ability but rather the encouragement 'that God may work by the meanest and poorest words, as well as by the most polished and ornate—yea, perhaps more readily, that the glory be all His own.' He saw it as a way of keeping him humble since his speech was probably not as polished as it might otherwise have been. His preparation was, at the same time, no less.

Travelling with Tully

If the time at Larbert and Dunipace was formative for his pattern of preaching, it was equally so for his pastoral visitation. Essential to travelling was his useful means of transport—his pony Tully, 'not a majestic creature but a useful beast.' His main pastoral district was Kinnairds. This was where Robert Bruce, one of the great leaders of the Reformation, was once the laird. He liked to recall that Larbert was where Robert Bruce ministered and he prayed that God's blessings on his work would be similar. Once more his diaries give the clue to his approach to visiting. They show how helpful had been the time he had spent visiting poor homes in

Above: Kinnaird Old Mansion

Edinburgh under Chalmers' direction while a divinity student. It had taught him to aim at visiting all in the geographical parish rather than simply those who were already in touch with the Christian community.

McCheyne aimed at visiting between 12 to 15 families each day that he went out on his calls. As he visited, he gave an invitation to gather in the evening for a meeting at which he addressed them together. So for example, he writes in his diary: 'Visiting in Carron-shore. Well received everywhere. Truly a pleasant labour. Cheered me much. Preached to them afterwards from Proverbs 1.' Another day he records, 'Visited thirteen families, and addressed them all in the evening in the school, on Jeremiah 1:4, 'Going and weeping.' In addition he visited the dying and the many that suffered industrial injuries and were seriously ill. Their need gave him a sense of urgency to share the gospel.

Robert matched meticulous care in preaching with equal care in keeping notebooks recording his visits. Every man or woman's circumstance was recorded, enabling him to remember them for the next visit and to pray for them. He would write things like: 'John Hunter, No. 22. He, not at home. She, stout woman with sensible face. Spoke of her four bairns dead; three beside her. Visit, 14 July 1836. "I stand at door and knock." Altogether a decent woman. Husband to be at meeting.' He was self-critical in his notes: 'Yesterday up in Dunipace. It would seem as if I were afraid to name the name of Christ. Saw many worldly people greatly needing a word in season, yet could not get up my heart to speak. What I did failed almost completely. I am not worthy, Lord!' Getting to know the people in and around Larbert coincided with necessary self-knowledge.

Foundations put in place

Although McCheyne's assistantship was short, it confirmed and established spiritual attitudes and disciplines that flourished in the years afterwards. His missionary concern did not diminish and he renewed his willingness to go abroad if called. He believed that all true ministers must show missionary commitment as proof of their calling. Alexander Duff preached close by at Stirling in April 1836 speaking with 'greater warmth and energy than ever'. McCheyne concluded, 'I am now made willing, if God shall open the way, to go to India. Here am I; send me!'

Early morning quiet times of prayer and Bible reading were the order for each day. He kept a prayer diary reminding him of people and subjects requiring his prayers, together with important scriptures to guide him. It was his habit to read or sing a psalm. After reading the Scriptures, he prayed in response to them, and engaged in intercession for his flock and friends.

McCheyne longed to grasp the whole range of God's revelation in the Bible, wanting to go beyond what was familiar to what was unfamiliar. His study of Jonathan Edwards continued, together with the letters of Samuel Rutherford–the renowned Puritan writer–which were often in his hand. He did not despise books of general knowledge either, because he found illustrations of spiritual truth in them that he could use in teaching and preaching.

Above: The River Carron at Dunipace **Centre, above:** *Alexander Duff*

Left: The clock of St Stephen's Church, Edinburgh, that McCheyne was possibly familiar with. It was a James Ritchie clock, with an unusually large pendulum

Below: Alexander Somerville, McCheyne's successor at Larbert and Dunipace, pictured in old age

While at Larbert and Dunipace McCheyne began to contribute articles to the Scottish *Christian Herald*, one of which was 'On Sudden Conversions', encouraging readers to expect them. A more important form of writing was his letter writing—a 19th century habit that he used for spiritual and pastoral purposes. In the time that remained to McCheyne, letters were to be an important ministry, especially when he was restricted because of illness.

What McCheyne missed most in rural Stirlingshire was regular contact with his Christian friends that had so marked his student years. On reflection he realised that fellowship of this sort had helped to keep him spiritually alert. He used a simple illustration. When in Edinburgh the chiming of its many clocks made him look instinctively at his watch. So when he met his friends and talked about his Saviour he intuitively checked his relationship to him. Now, not seeing his friends where he worked, he felt the danger of spiritual slackness. It was probably out of this awareness that at this time he and other young ministers covenanted to pray for one another on Saturday evenings with regard to their responsibilities of the next day.

The astonishing amount of experience compressed in the brief period of McCheyne's spiritual apprenticeship was clearly God's provision for him. When the time came for him to leave, huge congregations heard his last sermons at Larbert and Dunipace and he left them with regret. One consolation was that his friend Alexander Somerville was to be his successor.

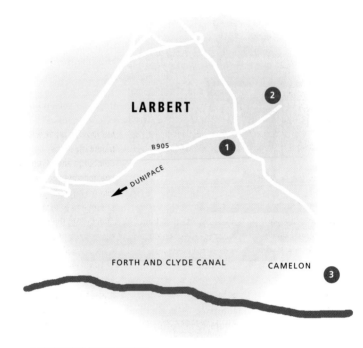

LARBERT

B905

DUNIPACE

FORTH AND CLYDE CANAL

CAMELON

1 LARBERT OLD PARISH CHURCH
2 LARBERT STATION
3 CAMELON (THE HUB OF THE FALKIRK
WHEEL AND CANAL OPERATIONS)

TRAVEL INFORMATION

Larbert

Larbert is within easy reach of both Glasgow (22 miles/36 km) and Edinburgh (30 miles or 46 kilometres) by car. By train it is usually a 30 to 40 minute journey from both Glasgow and Edinburgh, with a change sometimes necessary from Glasgow.

Larbert Old Parish Church

This is within a few minutes' walk from the station and was the original Larbert Church. The present building was built in 1820 and so was only 15 years old when McCheyne arrived. Notice the tower in which McCheyne held his class for young people, and visit the churchyard to see the grave of Robert Bruce. The headstone is to be found inside the church for the sake of its preservation.

Dunipace

The Dunipace Church where McCheyne ministered is now a block of flats and is situated almost exactly three miles from Larbert Old Parish Church. When you leave Larbert Old Parish Church Car Park you turn immediately to the left

Above: The Falkirk Wheel

and what was Dunipace Church is three miles on the left hand side. If you then continue on the same road it brings you into Dunipace itself with glimpses of the Carron River, so important for the earlier industries of the area.

The Falkirk Wheel

The Website provides full directions to the Wheel; although it is well sign-posted from whatever direction you approach Falkirk. An engineering and design wonder, this is the world's first and only rotating boat lift. It reconnects the Union Canal with the Forth and Clyde Canal, although they are 115ft apart, re-establishing east to west coast access for boats. Previously it required a series or 'flight' of 11 locks. It can lift 600 tonnes of water over 25 metres in less than four minutes, using the same energy as boiling just eight kettles of water. (www.thefalkirkwheel.co. uk).

Union Canal

The Edinburgh and Glasgow Union Canal was begun in 1818 and opened four years later in 1822. It crosses three major aqueducts and was intended to break the monopoly of the Edinburgh and Midlothian coal masters and mine owners by making it possible to transport coal directly into the city. When the Edinburgh and Glasgow Railway opened in 1842 the canal's profitability declined and it was finally abandoned in the 1960s. Since 2001 it has been reopened as part of the Millennium Link. At the city end, Edinburgh Quays is a major regeneration project with waterfront apartments, offices, shops and restaurants.

Above: Edinburgh Quays

❺ A young church and its first minister

Robert Murray McCheyne's call to a new church and congregation in Dundee provided a special opportunity for the development of his gifts and the expression of his convictions of what a local church should be like in its life and witness

The country district of Larbert suited well the vulnerable physical make-up of McCheyne. By contrast, Dundee, with its busy industry and population, was probably the worst possible location for him. His own natural preference was for a rural parish. But it was from Dundee that the call clearly came. A newly formed church—St Peter's—heard of him and he was one of six possible candidates, two of whom were his special friends, Andrew Bonar and Alexander Somerville. He preached as a candidate on 14 August 1836 and his text was the Song of Songs 2:8–17. His own view was that 'If the people have any sense, they will choose Andrew Bonar.' The elders' conviction, however, was different and they were more or less immediately persuaded that Robert was the man.

The date for his ordination and induction at Dundee was quickly arranged for 24 November 1836, led by John Roxburgh, the minister of St John's, in whose parish the new church was. His mentor at Larbert, John Bonar, introduced him to the people on

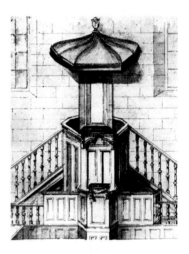

Above: A drawing of McCheyne's pulpit in St Peter's from a book entitled 'M'Cheyne from the Pew' by Kirkwood Hewart published in 1897, being the diary of William Lamb, one of McCheyne's elders

Facing page: St Peter's Church, Dundee, where McCheyne was minister from 1836 until his death

Dundee and the Industrial Revolution

The town of Dundee was growing at a tremendous rate when McCheyne began his ministry. Since 1780 its population had doubled, so that it was 56,000 and rising. The Firth of Tay provided a natural deep-water harbour, ideal for shipbuilding, and as a Whaling port it developed a prosperous maritime industry.

With a monopoly of the jute trade, this employed most of the population by the end of the century; the last jute mill closed in 1998. Jute became popular because flax was scarce, and the first jute carpeting was produced. Spinning and weaving employed women and children besides men. Steam-

driven mills were built in the town before the end of the 18th century and factories began to appear. The first power-loom factory was built in 1836 and some of the first railways were built in the Dundee area. The Dundee and Newryle Railway was opened in 1831, soon to be followed by the Dundee and Arbroath Railway begun in stages between 1848 and 1857. The variety of industry in Dundee made reasonably high wages possible with a proportionate amount of drunkenness. Second

only to Glasgow in drunkenness and crime, it is recorded that one parish had a single baker's shop and 108 public houses. This comparative affluence increased pastoral problems.

Above, left: Verdant Works courtyard, a jute mill opened in 1833 that operated until 1899

Above, right: Loading the Jute, Dundee Heritage Trust, Verdant Works

the following Sunday morning, and in the afternoon McCheyne preached his first sermon to them as their minister on Isaiah 61:1–3. His prayer was that the passage would be prophetic of the object of his arrival in Dundee. He learned later that people had been spiritually awakened by the sermon. He determined to commemorate the anniversary of his ordination by preaching on the same passage each year. On the Sunday evening his good friend, Andrew Bonar, preached. At the end of the day, McCheyne wrote, 'Felt given over to God, as one bought with a price.'

No magic attaches to ordination, since the laying on of the hands of ministers and elders is the acknowledgment of the call of God the Holy Spirit to a man to the ministry. But in McCheyne's

Right: Strawberry Bank, Dundee, where McCheyne first lived as minister at St Peter's

Right, below: Union Place, the second home of McCheyne and his sister in Dundee

case–no doubt because of the spiritual expectation God gave him–his ordination signalled a time of spiritual growth and the anticipation of increased strength and usefulness. These benefits were timely since much of the winter of 1836 was spent in visiting the unwell and dying on account of a flu epidemic.

The new pastor at St Peter's

The establishment of the new church within the original parish of St John's was the consequence of Dundee's growing population. St Peter's was the first church to be built at the west end of Dundee to cater for this growth. It was opened on 15 May 1836, and the first ten elders–known as the kirk session—were appointed from St John's, and became members of St Peter's. The new parish totalled nearly 4000 people, most of whom were weavers, warpers (those who arranged the yard on a loom), spinners, millwrights and labourers, plus some bankers, merchants and manufacturers. Like many new causes, the large building was plain and cheaply constructed, with a gallery on three sides and a seating capacity for 1175 people. It was to prove one of the most successful efforts at church extension—one of about 180 new churches between 1834 and 1838.

Settling into his new home in Dundee was immeasurably helped by Robert's unmarried sister, Elizabeth, who joined him to look after the life of the manse, first in Strawberry Bank and, from 1842, in Union Place, both side streets off the Perth Road. McCheyne's journal reveals the pattern of his devotional and working life. Rising each morning at 6.30, he spent two hours in prayer and meditation, a considerable amount of which was given to intercession, especially for the Jews. Self-examination was essential to his practice and for his personal benefit he wrote a guide to the subject entitled *Personal Examination and Reformation*. Breakfast was between 8.30 and 10 with family prayers.

Sermon preparartion

McCheyne read widely and profited particularly from Martin Luther, Jonathan Edwards, Richard Baxter and John Bunyan. Edward Fisher's *The Marrow of Modern Divinity* also greatly influenced him. Robert engaged in preliminary sermon preparation early in the week but the actual writing of his sermons usually began on Friday. Then on Saturday, he corrected and revised them with a view to committing their substance to memory. He took great trouble in writing them out, and once his text or passage was determined, he made a thorough exegesis of it, looking at the meaning of each word. This was followed by a paraphrase of the verse or passage in his own words. Pages of notes and observations followed as he pondered the material. If sermons by others were available on the same passage, he would then read them. He was not content until he could draw out three or four main points, followed by a full and complete outline, from which he could readily preach if need be.

Left:
McCheyne's Dundee: Old houses in Overgate

Above: Collessie, where McCheyne often escaped for quietness and solitude from his busy pastorate in Dundee

McCheyne aimed at simple and logical statements, sometimes using alliteration to make it easy for working class people to remember his main headings. Someone said, 'The heads of his sermons were not milestones that tell you how near you were to your journey's end, but they were nails which fixed and fashioned all he said. Divisions are often dry; but not so his divisions.' Basic to his preparation for preaching the Scriptures was the conviction that they 'All, all tell of Jesus—Jesus pervades the Bible—it is the standing witness to Jesus. ... The written Word testifies to the living Word.' One who listened to McCheyne preach Sunday by Sunday, tellingly testified that he did so in a 'kind and affectionate manner, and 'he draws you to Christ.'

The parish of St Peter's, at the west end of Dundee, was then on the edge of the countryside and McCheyne often escaped from the busy town to quiet rural places for times of prayer and meditation. Tully, his pony, went with him to Dundee and was particularly useful for such visits. The ruins of the church at Invergowrie was a favourite place. One day, for instance, he wrote in his diary, 'Rode to Collessie and Kirkcaldy. Sweet time alone in Collessie woods.' He felt meditation and prayer to be the foundation of his work.

The attention he gave to pastoral visitation in Larbert and Dunipace continued in Dundee. While in Larbert he usually called on twelve to fifteen families each visiting day, in Dundee this increased to twenty. He let the

The Catechism

This was the 17th century Westminster Shorter Catechism—the work of the Westminster Assembly, during the English Civil War between Charles I and Parliament that began in 1643. This Assembly prepared the Westminster Confession of Faith (one of the most influential creeds of Calvinism) the Larger and Shorter Catechisms, the Form of Church Government and the Directory for Public Worship. The Church of Scotland adopted the Westminster Standards in 1647, and McCheyne and his friends were loyal to them. The Shorter Catechism's 107 questions begin with the well-known question 'What is the chief end of man'? with the answer 'Man's chief end is to glorify God, and to enjoy him forever.'

families know the day beforehand of his intended visit, and always shared some part of the Scriptures and explained it. If there were children, he spoke to them, often examining them in the Catechism. As noted earlier, McCheyne kept careful records of all his visits, including the dates, the people he met, the Scriptures he read and the impressions he gained. He did not hesitate to speak plainly to those who were seriously ill and dying about their need to be ready for death. He thought it 'cruel kindness' to keep the truth of the seriousness of their need from them 'with murderous lies'. His object was not simply to get visits done but to see souls saved, and he visited not to discharge a responsibility or to obtain a good conscience but because he

delighted in it. As in Larbert, a special feature of this visitation was to invite all whom he visited in one day to an evening meeting in either a large home or a back green. These 'cottage lectures' could sometimes number nearly 200 people.

Sunday Services at St Peter's

From the beginning, McCheyne had a congregation of around 1100, with about a third coming from other parts of the town. The services were simple in format. Since McCheyne was musical, he often led the praise and felt that music was an integral part of praising God: 'There is perhaps none of the means of grace which is so much neglected by believers in the present day as that of singing praises to God.' He wanted the services to be as attractive as possible and to be marked by melodious and enthusiastic singing. To encourage the latter he held weekly meetings for singing during the summer months. Visitors described the singing at the services as 'very plain' but 'remarkably full and sweet'. McCheyne's favourite tune was Newington and it became known in the parish as McCheyne's tune.

By his public prayers he unconsciously taught his people how to pray. 'He never told us what prayer was,' one of them said, 'he never needed. Behold, he prayeth—that is prayer. Few that heard ever forgot his first two words "Holy Father".' He prayed extemporaneously although he frequently composed and prepared his thoughts beforehand.

Above: The High School Building at the end of Reform Street, Dundee

The words of Scripture guided and directed his prayers. Confession of sin was always present and his prayers were the outflow of his reverent fellowship with God and his urgent concern for God's honour and the interests of his people.

The reading of a passage of Scripture usually preceded his sermons. While his preaching was doctrinal, it was the Lord Jesus Christ whom he proclaimed. He wrote, 'It is strange how sweet and precious it is to preach directly about Christ, compared with all other subjects of preaching.' His Calvinism was as plain as his evangelistic zeal. He warmly preached the Lord Jesus as a gift laid down by the Father for every sinner to take freely. With outstanding winsomeness, he not only preached the gospel but he urged his hearers to receive it.

While McCheyne sometimes found it difficult to keep his sermons as short as he intended, he aimed at simplicity and used word pictures whenever possible, choosing the simpler word rather than the complicated. Basic to his understanding was his appreciation of the need for the work of the Holy Spirit as he preached to make it meaningful: 'We speak, it touches not. The Spirit takes it in hand, it lives—the living Word. Nothing so dead before—nothing so living now.'

The church programme and innovations

As early as 1837 McCheyne started a Sunday school—or 'Sabbath school' as it was called. They were not common at the time and little enthusiasm existed for them, but he recruited and trained the teachers and often prepared teaching notes for them. Robert aimed at having classes in all parts of the parish, and the average attendance in 1839 was 150. They met from six until eight on a Sunday evening. A children's worship service was also held at eight in the morning. He wrote hymns for them to sing and tracts and poems for them to read.

For young people over the age for Sunday school McCheyne arranged an evening class on a Tuesday with as many as 250 in attendance. His main topics were the Catechism and biblical subjects linked with informal discussion. Using his artistic gifts, the pastor illustrated his talks with drawings and objects of interest. Alongside this class he had one for young people who were showing by their faith a readiness to attend Communion. These endeavours saw no less than sixteen men from St Peter's enter the ministry.

As a new congregation, St Peter's had no traditions and this therefore provided scope for significant initiatives on the part of McCheyne. Most important was the weekly prayer meeting in the church. Having heard how meetings of this sort had been blessed in other places, he was keen to set up this regular coming together of God's people for prayer. Some of the most memorable times of his ministry were at the prayer meetings. He always opened briefly with a passage of Scripture calculated to stimulate prayer. After prayer he read something of the history of spiritual revivals to encourage his people to know how to pray for similar blessing. A comparable high point in the weekly schedule was the Thursday evening Bible Study, often to a full and overflowing church.

While elders were the norm in the churches, McCheyne's

Above: *McCheyne's home in 1839 in Strawberry Bank*

Above: The beginning of McCheyne's third pastoral letter to his congregation when he was convalescing at his parent's home in Edinburgh, written on 13 February 1839

expectations and training of elders were unusual. He insisted upon high qualifications and carefully defined duties. They were expected to replicate his own pastoral work. Besides encouraging his elders and deacons in the task of visiting, he established a system of deaconesses to help in the care of women and children. To be an elder was not simply an honour but a responsibility, especially in the corporate responsibility elders had for church discipline. McCheyne had not appreciated at the beginning of his ministry the importance of church discipline but his understanding of this aspect of pastoral responsibility grew.

Above: McCheyne's pulpit, accessible in St Peter's Church, although the pulpit is not now used

Left: McCheyne's Dundee: The Howff land in the heart of old Dundee granted to the Council for a graveyard in 1564. 'Howff' is a Scottish word for an inn or public house

Other helpful innovations to encourage reading and learning were a church library and, towards the end of his ministry, a yearly calendar for his people so that they could read the Old Testament once a year and the New Testament and the Psalms twice. This continues to be in print and is widely used. In addition McCheyne was keenly interested in the education of children and a school was erected for them—a relevant initiative in that in 1834 only one in thirteen of Dundee children received any education.

Developing interests and concerns

It is no exaggeration to say that McCheyne was involved in everything relating to gospel work in Dundee. Various societies set up for needy groups of people had his support as well as the Dundee Juvenile Bible and Missionary Society, the Dundee Tract Society and the Dundee Seaman's Society. He recognised the influence of newspapers for either good or evil and chose to contribute to them. Requests came to him to preach evangelistically on a weekday and to minister elsewhere at Communion weekends. Churches at Blairgowrie, Collace, Kirriemuir and Abernyte recalled memorable visits. In addition he continued to write for the Scottish *Christian Herald*.

McCheyne's concern for the Jewish people grew. A Jewish society had been formed in London in 1809, and in the General Assembly of the Church of Scotland in 1838 concerns for the Jews were expressed. In 1839 the Church of Scotland appointed a committee to discover the numbers, conditions and character of the Jewish people in Palestine and Europe, with a view to deciding how best their spiritual good could be served and the ideal places for mission stations. McCheyne was one of the committee of one hundred members. He wrote, 'To seek the

Above: Collessie Parish Church. It was in the woods nearby that McCheyne often spent time alone with God

lost sheep of the house of Israel is an object very near to my heart, as my people know it has ever been. Such an enterprise may probably draw down unspeakable blessings on the Church of Scotland, according to the promise, "they shall prosper who love thee."'

Calls from other churches and health alarm bells

McCheyne's reputation quickly spread. People heard of the crowds that flocked to his ministry and the positive innovations he had made. It has to be said too that some regarded his evangelical convictions with contempt and his success with perhaps jealousy. However, in less than a year he received three calls from other congregations, invitations attractive for their location and financial benefits. Some of his friends were inclined to encourage him to accept a country parish for the benefit of his health. His family certainly wished him to make a change. But Robert saw no reason to leave Dundee. He wrote, 'Happy the pastor who allows no hand but Christ's to place or to remove him. It is Christ alone who gives all ministers all their success.'

Consideration of McCheyne's weekly programme prompts the conviction that he worked extremely hard and probably too hard. Towards the end of 1838, particularly in the December, he was seriously ill with palpitations of the heart. His doctor advised him to rest, and to do so away from Dundee. The obvious place was his parents' home in Edinburgh. A benefit of this absence was a series of pastoral letters to his flock—yet another example of his deep pastoral care.

DUNDEE

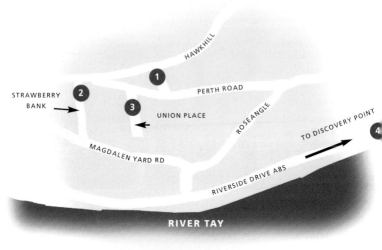

1 ST PETER'S CHURCH IN ST PETER'S STREET
2 STRAWBERRY BANK
3 UNION PLACE
4 DISCOVERY POINT

TRAVEL INFORMATION

Invergowrie

A village on the north shore of the Firth of Tay, it acts as a residential suburb of Dundee. Previously part of Dundee, it now lies within the Perth and Kinross council area. In the ancient churchyard are two large stones known as the Ewes (or Yowes) of Gowrie. Invergowrie toll-house stands nearby on the south side of the former Perth-Dundee turnpike road. The ancient ruins of

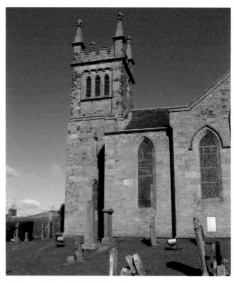

Above: Collessie Parish Church

Dargie Church are said to be the oldest Christian Church north of the River Tay.

St Peter's Free Church

St Peter's belongs to the Free Church of Scotland and is found in St Peter's Street, off the Perth Road. Its web-site provides a helpful history and news of its present congregation.

Manse sites: Strawberry Bank and Union Place Neither manse sites can now be seen. Strawberry Bank is an interesting lane whereas there is nothing really to see in Union Place as this has been subject to redevelopment. The old manse in Strawberry Bank was demolished towards the end of 1907 to make room for a rope factory, although the contractor took a photograph of it before taking it down. (www.stpeters-dundee.org.uk).

Collessie

An attractive and picturesque hamlet with narrow lanes in N E Fife, it is situated on a minor road just north of the A91, 5 miles (8 km) west of Cupar. Its ancient Parish Church (rebuilt 1838–1839) stands on a hillock at the centre of a settlement containing several well-preserved 17th, 18th, and 19th century weaving cottages, some with thatched roofs. The woods through which McCheyne used to walk are not now identifiable.

Dundee Tourist Information

Full information can be found on the websites (www.angusanddundee.co.uk) and (enquiries@angusand-dundee.co.uk).

Above: St Peter's Free Church from an old engraving

⑥ A great adventure

McCheyne was an unexpected member of a delegation to Palestine although he proved to be its most influential. The expedition caught the imagination of the Scottish people and produced one of the most fascinating travel documents of the 19th century. It prompted widespread spiritual concern for the Jews

The year 1839 began with Robert, off sick, staying with his parents in Edinburgh. Like many others he had been delighted at the decision of the Church of Scotland's General Assembly in 1838 to appoint a committee to see what could be done to help the Jewish people. His journal shows how regularly the Jews had a place in his prayers. The newly appointed committee decided to send a deputation to examine the state of Jews in Palestine and some of the European cities en route.

Dr Robert Candlish, later to be the successor to Thomas Chalmers as the leader of the Free Church of Scotland, was a driving force of the committee. C. H. Spurgeon, the popular London preacher of the time, spoke of Candlish warmly: 'A man hardly needs anything beyond Candlish. He is devout, candid, prudent and forcible.' An outstanding gospel preacher, he was minister at the time of St George's Church in Edinburgh and later became Principal of New College, Edinburgh, where ministers are still trained for the ministry.

Above: Dr Robert Candlish, one of the most influential ministers in the Church of Scotland, and later the Free Church

Facing page: The Wailing Wall in Jerusalem

Andrew Bonar (1810–1892)

Andrew Bonar was the younger brother of Horatius Bonar, the author of many well-known hymns such as *I heard the voice of Jesus say*. His education was identical and parallel with McCheyne's. Licensed to preach in July 1835, he served his assistantship at Jedburgh. He was ordained at Collace, near Perth, in September 1838 and many years later in 1878 became Moderator of the Free Church General Assembly. His continuing influence has been through his biography of Robert Murray McCheyne (Bonar pictured right).

Candlish was totally committed to missionary enterprise.

A surprising suggestion

Walking one day with Robert in Edinburgh, Dr Candlish suggested to him that he might like to be one of the party deputed to go to Palestine. The suggestion came as a surprise since Robert was only twenty-five and was convalescing before returning to his ministry in Dundee. He was not yet physically strong, but his concern for the Jewish people made such a possibility immediately attractive and exciting, especially as his closest friend, Andrew Bonar, was to be a member of the party.

McCheyne's doctors immediately supported the idea of the overseas trip. They felt the sea air and the warmer climate would aid his recovery. His flock at St Peter's, although naturally alarmed at the news to begin with, were reassured both by the doctors' convictions and by the appointment of William Burns to stand in for McCheyne.

Left: David Dickson (left) and Robert Candlish (right) in 1839

Above: Andrew Bonar

Above: *Corstorphine Hill—one of McCheyne's favourite walks in Edinburgh*

And so it was that Robert and Andrew joined two senior ministers—Dr Alexander Black, a theological Professor who was good at languages, and Dr Alexander Keith, known for his winsome character and actions—to conduct the investigation. The committee provided a list of questions for them to answer to help determine the real condition and attitudes of the Jewish people and to suggest how and where the church might plan and operate a Jewish mission in Palestine and Europe.

An adventurous journey

27 March 1839 marked the beginning of McCheyne's journey as he sailed for London to prepare the way in advance of the other members of the deputation. The journey took approximately 41 hours from Dundee to London. Arriving in London, they quickly discovered that interest in their mission was not limited to Scotland. The office-bearers and members of the London Jewish Society, and other Christian friends in the city, showed considerable interest and

Above: 20 Hill Street, Edinburgh, the home of McCheyne's parents in 1839

Below: The interior of the National Scotch Church in Regent Square, London in 1839

kindness; the Religious Tract Society provided publications in various languages. At the National Scotch Church in Regent Square, London (now the Regent Square Church near what we now know as King's Cross and St Pancras), they were commended to God the night before they set off for Dover to begin their journey abroad on 12 April.

The total itinerary was to take six months in three unequal legs: first, across southern Europe, second, by ship to Alexandria in Egypt and, third, by camel from Egypt to Palestine. It was something of an adventure when we remember that although Thomas Cook was born five years before McCheyne, he did not open his travel office in London until twelve years after McCheyne's death. They were limited in how far they could plan ahead. Their letters home were published in both the national and the foreign press and they kept a careful diary

Left: The Regent Square Church today

of every place they visited and the impressions they formed.

Once in France the travellers made for Paris and visited tourist sites like the Champs Elysées, the Church of the Magdalene, the Palaces and the Pillar in the Place Vendome. Dismayed at the crowds shopping on a Sunday in the Champs Elysées, they were delighted to find fellowship in the Marbeuf Chapel in Rue Marbeuf, just off that famous thoroughfare, and in the evening they heard a sermon by Frédéric Monod. In every place the deputation visited, they enquired about the Jews, visited where possible any Jewish synagogues, and endeavoured to bear witness to Christ through the Old Testament Scriptures. Monod told them that sadly he knew of no real conversion of Jews in Paris.

The party used an interesting variety of transport in their journeys. In France, until they reached Saône in Burgundy, they made use of a diligence, a form of four-wheeled stagecoach. Then they took steam boats to Marseilles and onwards from there by steamers to Egypt, via Genoa, Leghorn and Malta. They completed their journey across Sinai to Jerusalem on camels. Dr Black fell from his camel in Sinai and did not really recover from the fall throughout his travels.

Thieves and robbers

The dangers and hazards they met in their travels read like the apostle Paul's accounts of his own in 2 Corinthians 11. Nevertheless, they felt God's protecting hand as they were delivered from thieves and robbers. McCheyne walked one Sunday to a quiet spot where two shepherds came and sat down beside him. After trying to talk with them by signs, he rose to leave but they refused to let him pass and forced him into woods. A desperate struggle followed for about a quarter of an hour until McCheyne lay on the ground exhausted. Suddenly, for no apparent reason, they left him there without robbing him.

Mosque of Omar

Built on the site of the Temple, the Dome of the Rock was built by the Muslim ruler Abd el-Malik in 688–691. In McCheyne's time a lead dome covered it but it was replaced with an anodised aluminium gold-coloured covering in 1965 and replaced again in 1993 with a gold covering. Muslims believe it is the place where Abraham was prepared to sacrifice Isaac.

Mosquitoes continually dogged their path, many places in which they stayed were vermin-infested, and plague raged in Egypt and Palestine. At one stage McCheyne became desperately ill on board ship with no medical help at hand.

A time to be remembered

Great excitement surrounded their arrival in Jerusalem on 7 June 1839—a day they reckoned to be among the most eventful of their lives. McCheyne was the first to dismount from his camel and hurry on foot until he reached a point where the city came in sight. 'Soon, all of us were on the spot,' they recorded, 'buried in thought, and wistfully gazing on the wondrous scene where the Redeemer died. The nearer we came to the city, the more we felt it a solemn thing to be where "God manifest in the flesh" had walked. The feelings of that hour could not even be spoken. We all moved

Above: Rue Marbeuf where McCheyne and his party found fellowship in the Marbeuf Chapel

Left: The Champs Elysées in Paris

Left McCheyne described his journey on a camel as feeling like floating or sailing in the air

forward in silence, or interchanging feelings only by a word.'

Like today's visitors to the Holy Land they went to places like the Church of the Holy Sepulchre, the Mosque of Omar, the Citadel of David, the Temple Wall, the Pool of Siloam, the Mount of Olives, Gethsemane, Bethany, Capernaum and Bethlehem. Their visit to the grotto at Bethlehem understandably upset them because they felt that what professed to be respect for something sacred really dishonoured the truth, and the Church of the Holy Sepulchre was a similar disappointment and they were convinced that it was not the true site. General Gordon did not discover what we now know as the Garden Tomb and Gordon's Calvary until 1883.

Bethany and Gethsemane proved to be the two most meaningful places to McCheyne and his colleagues. They wrote of Bethany: 'Perhaps there was no scene in the Holy Land which afforded us more unmingled enjoyment.' Of Gethsemane McCheyne and Bonar recorded, 'Early one morning two of us set out to visit Gethsemane … we soon came to the low rude wall enclosing the plot of ground which for ages has borne the name of Gethsemane. Clambering over we examined the sacred spot and its eight olive-trees. These are very large and very old, but their branches are still strong and vigorous …We read over all the passages of Scripture relating to Gethsemane, while seated there together. … Each of us occupied part of the time alone—in private meditation—and then we joined together in prayer—putting our sins into that cup which our Master drank here, and pleading for our own souls, for our far distant friends, and for the flocks committed to our care.'

Decision time and disturbing news

The continued ill-health of Dr Black, not only as a result of his

The Auchterarder case

Auchterarder is in Perthshire, near Gleneagles, today Scotland's foremost luxury hotel. The issue was over the right of congregations to call ministers whom they chose, rather than a patron presenting a minister of his personal choice. 'Was the Lord Jesus King in his own church or not?' was the question many asked. Events in Scotland were moving towards the break that occurred in 1843—after McCheyne had died—when over 450 ministers left the Church of Scotland to form the Free Church of Scotland.

fall but also because of the climate, led eventually to their unanimous decision to divide into two groups, with the two older men returning home via Constantinople and the Danube. Later they all came to recognise God's providence in this decision in that as McCheyne and Bonar resumed their travels in Palestine, the two older men's journey resulted in a Scots mission to Budapest. The two younger men reached Galilee through South Lebanon with a brief stop in Sidon. They then returned home by way of the Bosphorus, Moldavia, Wallachia (Romania) and Austrian Poland.

Correspondence with Scotland throughout the journey was understandably difficult. From Leghorn in Italy and Breslau in Prussia McCheyne wrote letters addressed to his flock in Dundee and like his other letters they are an example of pastoral care at its best. When they were in Jerusalem they received on Saturday 15 June, with great excitement, the first letters from home since their departure. Refreshed and encouraged by them, they were

Above: Jerusalem and The Mosque of Omar

Above: The excavated ruins of the synagogue at Capernaum

also disturbed at the news that the Auchterarder case had been decided against the church in the House of Lords. They sensed that a trial of faith was ahead of them in Scotland.

A mission among the Jews

No doubt exists about the value of their months away. By the end of their journey they had formed clear impressions and arrived at definite conclusions and recommendations. Their journey through France and Italy had provided valuable information about Jews in both countries. With Jews so scattered in France, they suggested that an itinerant missionary would be the most valuable first approach, and someone who had an in-depth knowledge of Jewish learning. They decided that Leghorn, in Tuscany, was the most promising station for placing a missionary

Above: The Garden Tomb, Jerusalem

Above: Bethany in the 19th century

among Jews in Italy with others placed elsewhere where they could serve Protestants as well as reach out to Jews.

Jews in Palestine proved somewhat unwilling to disclose their true numbers although the deputation kept careful statistics about what they found in every place they visited and of any signs of missionary activity. Their conclusion was that Palestine had a total Jewish population of 10,000 to 12,000, with about 6,000 to 7,000 Jews living in Jerusalem. Few young men went to Palestine and those Jews who did were generally elderly. Their poverty was great and numerous quarrels divided them. The deputation saw

First-fruits of the Jewish Mission

Adolph Saphir (1831–1891) was born in Budapest, the son of a Jewish merchant. He and his family were converted through the Jewish Mission of the Church of Scotland. He studied at the Free Church College in Edinburgh and served as a missionary to the Jews in Hamburg and also as a Presbyterian minister in England. Alfred Edersheim (1825–1889), born of Jewish parents in Vienna, came under the influence of 'Rabbi' John Duncan when Duncan was chaplain to workmen on the Danube bridge at Pesth (Budapest).

Edersheim later went to Scotland and Berlin to study, becoming a Presbyterian minister in 1846 and missionary to the Jews at Jassy, Romania. After three years he returned to Britain. A prolific writer, his most influential work was his *Life and Times of Jesus the Messiah,* a book still widely used today.

the necessity of a missionary knowing more languages than Hebrew and the wisdom of sending one good missionary rather than fifty unsuitable ones. They recommended Galilee as the ideal place for a Scots Mission to be set up because of its congenial climate, with summers in the hills and mild winters by the Sea of Galilee. However, they were convinced that more urgent than the need of the Jews in Palestine was that of the thousands of Jews scattered throughout Europe.

Revival at home and a best-selling book

As McCheyne and Bonar put together their report, little did they know how wonderfully God was answering their prayers for Scotland in their absence. During the last leg of their return journey, when they arrived in Hamburg, the port from which they were to sail for England, news reached them of the revival taking place in St Peter's, Dundee—under the ministry of William Burns! As they pondered this exciting news, they wondered if one of the providential causes of this longed-

Above: Jerusalem—the wailing wall

Below: McCheyne's drawing of a Sycamore tree

for revival was the enthusiasm focused on the Mission to the Jews; it had long been their conviction that a concern for missions—especially to the Jews—would bring new life to God's cause in Scotland. Later, at the Church of Scotland Assembly in 1840, McCheyne drew attention to the 'remarkable fact' that at the time the Mission was in Palestine: 'God visited His people in Scotland, by giving them bread in a way unknown since the days of Cambuslang and Moulin.' Both Cambuslang in South Lanarkshire, near Glasgow in 1742 and Moulin in Perthshire near Pitlochry in 1799 had witnessed outstanding periods of revival.

In 1842 the Church of Scotland published the account of their journey—The Narrative of a Visit to the Holy Land and Mission of Enquiry to the Jews. 23,000 copies were in print by 1847. The more than thirty drawings it contains were by McCheyne and the narrative was mainly the work of Andrew Bonar, although they each cooperated in its writing.

The impact of The Narrative upon the Scottish church and the wider church was immense. The Committee that sent them was authorised 'to take steps for preparing and sending missionaries to the stations most promising', and the General Assembly recommended that collections be made throughout the church for this object. The effect was felt first in Europe with missionaries sent to Poland and Hungary. The establishment of the Scottish Mission in Palestine took place much later in 1885.

Above: A drawing by McCheyne of the remains of an ancient synagogue
Top: A Jewish family in mid 19th century Jerusalem reflecting their elderly nature

Above: A tall ship at Hamburg Docks. It was here at Hamburg that the returning party received news of the revival in Dundee

Lasting fruit

Once home, both McCheyne and Bonar quickly engaged in active deputation among the churches sharing news of their trip and concern for the Jews. McCheyne went to Ireland in July 1840 and spoke in Belfast and Dublin. Missionaries from the Presbyterian Church in Ireland went out in 1841. The deputation's original longing had been to stir up the church to love the Jews, and there were encouraging evidences of their success. Fifty years later at the 1889 Free Church General Assembly, those who had come to Christ through the Mission to the Jews gave moving testimony to its success. News of the progress of the work in Tiberias and in New York, the latter by a young Jew brought to Christ by one of their missionaries in Breslau, Poland, increased the thanksgiving.

Above: *It was in the Marbeuf Chapel that McCheyne first worshipped on the Sunday he was in Paris. In the evening he listened to a sermon by Frédéric Monod (1794–1863) the French Protestant pastor of the Oratoire Church in Paris, who founded the Union of the Evangelical Churches of France*

TRAVEL INFORMATION

Hill Street

The first main road parallel with Princes Street is George Street. Travelling from Charlotte Square, the first turning left along George Street is Castle Street, and Hill Street is the first street on the right.

Corstorphine Hill

Corstorphine Hill is on the west side of Edinburgh, behind the Edinburgh Zoo. The Zoo is the best place to get off a bus for the hill. On the same side as the Zoo is Kaimes Road, a steep climb that leads to the hill. Buses 12, 26 and 31 go to the Zoo.

New College

New College is at the top of the Mound, close to the Waverley Station, the principal Edinburgh Railway Station.

London

The National Scotch Church in Regent Square

This was one of several churches serving the many Scots living in London. It had been built as a result of the ministry of Edward Irving because the church building where he first ministered in London became too small. Sadly, Irving became sidetracked from the fundamentals of the gospel and was

disciplined and removed from office (see page 38). At the time of McCheyne's visit, the minister was the Revd. Peter MacMorland, soon to be followed by James Hamilton, a good friend of McCheyne's. Now known as Regent Square United Reformed Church, the address is now Tavistock Place— close to London's Euston Station. The original building was destroyed in the Second World War in February 1945, with the loss of ten lives.

Paris

The Champs Elysées is the main street and broad avenue in Paris with the impressive Arc de Triomphe at its end. The Arc de Triomphe commemorates Napoleon

Bonaparte's victories. Its erection was completed just three years before McCheyne's visit.

Rue Marbeuf

The nearest Metro stations to the Rue Marbeuf are Alma Marceau and Franklin D. Roosevelt and they are within sight of the Arc de Triomphe on the Champs Elysées. No trace, however, of Marbeuf Chapel remains.

Israel

Travel in Israel is best achieved by joining one of the many tours, all of which will aim to include the principal places McCheyne and his colleagues visited. The Israel Ministry of Tourism has an impressive web site and includes a virtual tour (www.goisrael.com).
☎ (020) 7299 1100

Eglise Reformee de L'Oratoire du Louvre

It was here in 1838 that McCheyne and his party listened to a sermon by Frédéric Monod.
145, rue Saint-Honoré
75001 PARIS.
Nearest Metro : Louvre Rivoli.

Above: *A street market in Jerusalem*

Below: *Eglise Reformee de L'Oratoire du Louvre*

❼ Revival at St Peter's

The spiritual awakening that took place at St Peter's during McCheyne's absence in Palestine continued on his return. It was a tremendous encouragement to all who had been looking for God to work in this unique way and was wide in its influence

The news that reached McCheyne in Hamburg of the revival taking place in St Peter's served to increase his eagerness and excitement at returning to his flock. He and Andrew Bonar pondered the connection between the concern of the church in Scotland for the Jews and the answer to their prayers for revival. We are not in a position to be dogmatic about the truth of that possible link. There can be little doubt that the people's expectation and prayer for it had been helped by the history of revivals that McCheyne had read to them at the weekly prayer meetings, together with his sermons on the subject. In July 1838, preaching on Isaiah 44:3, 4, he began by saying, 'These words describe a time of refreshing. There are no words in the whole Bible that have been oftener in my heart and oftener on my tongue than these, since I began my ministry among you. And yet, although God has never, from the first day, left us without some tokens of his presence, he has never fulfilled this promise; and I have taken it up today, in order that we may consider it more fully, and plead it more anxiously with God.'

McCheyne returned to Dundee

Above: *William Burns in national costume as a missionary in China*

Facing page: *The Steeple Church, Dundee. The tower is the oldest part of the church and dates from the 15th century*

Above: McCheyne's St Andrew's Church, Dundee

on November 23 1839 and the next day he met with William Burns. This coincided with the day of the weekly prayer meeting and Robert and William went together into the pulpit. He was amazed to see the church completely filled in a way he had never witnessed before. The sight overwhelmed him. Not a seat was unoccupied, the aisles were filled and the stairs up to the pulpit were crowded either with the elderly or the children. He read Psalm 66 and the singing seemed to him 'tender and affecting, as if the people felt that they were praising a present God.' After prayer with them, he preached for more than an hour from 1 Corinthians 2:1–4, not telling them about his journey to

The revival at St Peter's

In the history of the church, revivals stand out as one of the great means by which God has kept his work alive. Although human instruments are important, the only explanation for such a special work is God's power and in particular that of his Holy Spirit. Christians are renewed, quickened and stirred to pray and to share their faith with those who are unconverted. The Bible is always central and its preaching leads to conviction of sin and conversion. In written testimony to a committee of the Church of Scotland, McCheyne testified, 'I have myself frequently seen the preaching of the word attended with so much power, and eternal things brought so near that the feelings of the people could not be restrained. I have observed at such times an awful and breathless stillness pervading the assembly; each hearer bent forward in the posture of rapt attention … I have myself once or twice seen the service in the house of God continue till about midnight. On these occasions the emotion during the preaching of the word was so great, that after the blessing had been pronounced at the usual hour, the greater part of the people remained in their seats or occupied the passages, so that it was impossible to leave them. In consequence of this, a few words more were spoken suited to the state of awakened souls; singing and prayer filled up the rest of the time. In this way the meeting was prolonged by the very necessity of the case.'

Above: *St Andrew's Church, Dundee, today*

Palestine but showing them the way of salvation. Never had he preached to such an audience, with so many weeping and waiting for God's word to be spoken. Coming out of the church afterwards, the road to his home was crowded with old and young, waiting to welcome him back. Before they would disperse he had to preach and pray with them. In the days that followed he was able to learn of all the events surrounding the revival, together with its evidences and its continuance.

The human instrument

McCheyne's hesitancy about leaving St Peter's to go to Palestine had been relieved when William Burns was found to be available as his locum. That choice was clearly demonstrated to be God's will. Burns proved to be the principal instrument, humanly speaking, for the awakening that took place. His first months at St Peter's had seemed uneventful, and from April to July of 1839 he preached with no particular results, although there is impressive testimony to the ardour, energy and true eloquence of his preaching. He was very conscious of 'being in a field so richly watered and blessed'. Later on he admitted that in these early months he had shrunk from alarming the people by making them face up to their spiritual need.

'*The Man with the Book*'

FIRST PIONEER OF THE E.P. MISSION

REVEREND

WILLIAM CHALMERS BURNS, M.A.

William Burns

Two years younger than McCheyne, born in Duns, Angus, Burns studied law at Aberdeen and divinity at Glasgow. As a probationer minister, licensed to preach in 1839, he committed himself to missionary service in India but as there were no openings at the time, he was free to assist at St Peter's. Ultimately he was to work as a missionary in China with the Presbyterian Church of England, preceding Hudson Taylor's arrival there to whom he proved an inspiration. He translated hymns and *Pilgrim's Progress* into Chinese.

Above: A page from 'Working His Purpose Out'. The history of the English Presbyterian Mission 1847–1947 by Edward Band, published in 1965

The progress of revival

The revival began not in Dundee but in Kilsyth in July 1839. Returning from the funeral of his brother-in-law in Paisley, Burns stopped off at Kilsyth on his return to Dundee to assist his father, a parish minister, for the communion season; the practice was to surround the Communion Sunday with a number of teaching and preaching services. His father had been the minister in Kilsyth since April 1821 and had shown interest in the subject of revival and encouraged his elders to pray for it.

The revival in Kilsyth began on the Tuesday and the effects were dramatic. All business in the town stopped and daily services for prayer and preaching were held in the churches for the following three months. An eyewitness wrote, 'The web became nothing to the weaver, nor the forge to the blacksmith, nor his bench to the carpenter, nor his furrow to the ploughman. They forsook all to crowd the churches and the prayer-meetings. There were nightly sermons in every church, household meetings for prayer in every street, twos and threes in earnest conversation on every road, and single wrestlers with God in the solitary places of the field and glen.' Burns, assisted by his father and other ministers, preached to crowds of three or four thousand. Interested and merely curious people travelled by train from Glasgow to witness what was happening and to hear the preaching. For the celebration of communion in September, attendances were estimated at between 12,000 and 15,000.

On 8 August Burns returned to St Peter's and preached two days later at the regular prayer meeting. At the end of the service he explained why he had been

delayed in his return. He invited any who wished to hear more about salvation to remain behind. Around a hundred remained and after he had spoken to them 'suddenly the power of God seemed to descend, and all were bathed in tears.' The following night, 11 August, another meeting took place with similar results and many professing conversion: 'It was like a pent-up flood breaking forth; tears were streaming from the eyes of many, and some fell to the ground, groaning, and weeping, and crying for mercy.' For four months meetings were held almost every night at St Peter's, with great crowds and multiplying prayer meetings. On his return from Palestine, McCheyne found thirty-nine such meetings in the congregation. Sermons revolved around the formula: ruin by the fall, righteousness by Christ and regeneration by the Spirit. Much time was taken up in private interviews with enquirers.

McCheyne rejoiced in all that he found had happened, although it cannot have been easy at first for him to discover that the revival had taken place during his absence. Some feared that a jealous spirit might exist among the congregation, some saying, 'I am of McCheyne' and others 'I of Burns', but these fears proved groundless in that both men tried their hardest to have no desire but the salvation of men and women. The relationship between them was warm and friendly. In a letter to Burns, McCheyne wrote, 'I shall never be able to thank you for all your labours among the precious souls committed to me.' He reported to Andrew Bonar, 'Everything here I have found in a state better than I expected.' He and Burns shared the preaching and Robert wrote to Andrew, 'His views of divine truth are clear and commanding. There is a great deal of substance in what he preaches, and his manner is very powerful—so much so, that he sometimes made me tremble. In private he is deeply prayerful, and seems to feel his danger of falling into pride.'

The revival continued after McCheyne's return. The primary means was the preaching of the word of God and the counselling that followed. He knew increased liberty in proclaiming the gospel and the constant expectation of seeing people converted as a result. Little notes are to be found at the beginning or the end of his sermon manuscripts, 'Master, help!' 'Help, Lord, help!' 'Send showers.' 'Pardon, give the Spirit, and take the glory.' 'May the opening of my lips be right things!' He typically records in his diary one night that twenty anxious souls had been talking with him. He sometimes set apart an evening for the purpose of meeting with those who were seeking salvation. One notebook records four hundred visits that he made to enquirers in the course of that year and the years following.

Every part of Dundee society was affected, and as many men as women—although the wealthy were least affected. Special meetings were not held for children but they were equally influenced and young children even had their own prayer meetings. People who had been believers before the revival, benefited from it also. Besides being confirmed in their faith, they showed a far greater appreciation of God's word and an awareness of their

Left McCheyne's Vestry at St Peter's

Left: St Peter's Church from the Perth Road

own need and the loveliness of Christ. McCheyne wrote, 'At a time of revival believers get a deeper and more awful discovery of the pollution of their own hearts; they get such a view of the volcano within that they are brought to Christ with enlarged views; they are brought to see him, it may be, as Thomas did, when he exclaimed, "My Lord and my God." They are brought to see, to an extent they did not see before, the power, the love, and the beauty of Christ.'

Lasting fruit

As in all periods of revival there was some backsliding of those he had regarded as really converted, and also among those who had come under conviction without making a profession of faith. His understanding, along with that of his colleagues, was that those who turned back were those who had never really believed. Every revival reveals the flaws of human nature and McCheyne expected this; however, he testified that he did not meet 'one case of extravagance or false fire, although doubtless there may be many.'

The revival had its detractors and some tried to discredit it. A principal Dundee paper was–and remains–the *Courier*. In its issue on 17 September 1839 it categorised those meeting in St Peter's as follows: '(1) People of small brains, little or no judgment, and perhaps too much nervous susceptibility; (2) people who had a craving for excitement; (3) idlers; (4) the curious

… who go for the novelty;
(5) indiscriminate church-goers, "who go from a sort of mania"; (6) "few, like us, who go to see what is the matter".' These criticisms were repeated in *The Scotsman* in the days that followed. They were perhaps inevitable and the best answer to them was transformed lives.

Even though the danger is always present that people may equate spiritual blessing with the messenger rather than the message and its source, McCheyne never left his people in doubt: 'Who is the author in a work of grace?' he asked. 'It is God: "I will pour." It is God who begins a work of anxiety in dead souls. … If any of you have been awakened, and made to beat upon the breast, it is God and God alone, that has done it. If ever we are to see a widespread concern among your families—children

Above: McCheyne's Dundee: The Strathmartine lodgings for the upper classes

Above: 'The Dundee Courier' building. The paper was established in 1801

asking their parents—parents asking their children—people asking their ministers, "What must I do to be saved?" … God must pour out the Spirit.'

Many journeys and visits

While the first phase of the revival centred on Kilsyth and Dundee, the second phase surrounded the activities of a number of men who visited numerous parishes in Scotland and then further afield. Perth, Blairgowrie, Dumbarney, Breadalbane, Collace, Ancrum, Kelso, Jedburgh, Aberfeldy, Tarbet, Tain, Glasgow and other places were touched by it. Denominational barriers were broken down and believers felt, as they had never experienced before, their oneness in Christ. Among the principal characters were

William Burns, McCheyne, and his close friends, Alexander Somerville and the Bonar brothers. The leaders were for the most part younger men in their thirties or younger. Not having his own parish, Burns did the most travelling and tended to work on his own while the others made visits in pairs or groups. At one meeting in Perth about 150 people came under conviction of sin and more than 200 came in the morning of the next day to seek spiritual counsel. This awakening proved to be the beginning of a solid work of grace in Perth. Other districts were soon sharing in the blessing. Burns urged McCheyne to give up being a parish minister to engage in itinerant evangelism and the suggestion was not without its

Below: The Imposing neo-classical Sheriff Courthouse in Dundee designed by George Angus in 1833

attraction. McCheyne wrote to his sister, 'I think God will yet make me a wandering minister.'

It has been suggested that the revival of 1839 was the herald and preparation for the even more extensive awakening of 1859. There seems little doubt that the publication of Andrew Bonar's biography of McCheyne and the account it gives of the revival in Dundee stirred up many to pray for similar blessing.

Above: McCheyne's Dundee: The High Street and Luckenbooth ('locked booths', housing the first permanent shops)

The Jewish Mission

It would have been understandable if the preoccupations of the revival had precluded other previous concerns. But the Jewish mission continued to be important to McCheyne. He travelled on deputation in its interests to meetings whether large or small. In Forfar he spoke to 'a small band of friends of the Jews' whereas in Glasgow in St George's Church 'to a very crowded assembly in behalf of Israel. Was helped to speak plainly to their own consciences.' He visited his fellow Presbyterians in Ireland at their invitation and awakened a deep interest in the cause of the Jews.

Above: The Town Hall (1816) at Kelso, the town in which one of Robert Murray McCheyne's close friends, Horatius Bonar, became minister in 1837. Bonar left in 1866 to become minister of Chalmers Memorial Church, Edinburgh

Dundee

Verdant Works, West Henderson's Wynd, Dundee DD1 5BT.

The Museum of Dundee's Industrial History and European Industrial Museum of the Year in 1999. An invaluable insight into the industrial history of Dundee and how the social classes lived together in 19th century Dundee. There is not a bus service that goes directly to it but a number 22 stops close by, at Blackness Road. It lies less than 15 minutes walk from the train station and is clearly sign-posted. There is wheelchair access. (www.verdantworks.com).

His Majesty's Frigate Unicorn

Built with 46 guns for the Royal Navy in the Chatham dockyard, and launched in 1824. One of the most successful ship designs of the period. It is less than ten minutes walk from the Railway Station, following the river-front walkway. (www.frigateunicorn.org).

Above: Verdant Works entrance

Below: The home page of Verdant Works website, Dundee

RRS Discovery

Situated at Discovery Point, just a few minutes from both the Rail Station and the Bus Station, is Captain Scott's famous ship RRS Discovery, built in Dundee. It was one of the last wooden three-masted ships to be built in Britain and the first to be constructed specifically for scientific research. Launched in 1901 it was the beginning of an adventure that would take her deep into the unknown waters of Antarctica and secure her a significant place in the history of polar exploration. The Discovery Point Centre is fully accessible to wheelchair users. The area below deck on the ship, however, is not suitable for wheelchairs but there is a video presentation booth available on the quayside. (www.rrsdiscovery.com).

Above: *His Majesty's Frigate Unicorn*

Top: *RRS Discovery*

8 Suddenly cut off

The revival in St Peter's that began in 1839 continued and was consolidated. Preaching opportunities elsewhere multiplied and McCheyne became heavily involved in the politics of the Church of Scotland. The shadow of the imminent disruption increased. McCheyne's death took everyone by surprise

From the beginning of his ministry, both at Larbert and Dundee, periods of illness and weakness troubled McCheyne. Illness had preceded his visit to Palestine and while there he was seriously ill. The bouts of sickness seem to have increased in number in the years that followed his return from Palestine. The pastor himself was aware of his heart's alarming palpitations. Letters to William Burns refer to his feelings of weakness. One incident—and accident—occurred that may have accentuated his weakness: McCheyne was engaged in deputation with Thomas Guthrie in Forfarshire in the interests of Church Extension, and they received hospitality in the home in Errol of the minister James Grierson. Gymnastic equipment was set up in the garden for the use of the family. Always ready to join in with young people, and an enthusiast for gymnastics, Robert took part, rushing at a horizontal bar resting on the forks of two upright poles and he went through a series of athletic manoeuvres. As he hung by his heels some five or six feet above the ground, the bar

Above: Thomas Guthrie in 1841

Facing page: The Wishart Arch gained its name from the Reformer George Wishart (1513–46). Wishart used it as a pulpit to preach during the plague of 1544

Thomas Guthrie (1803–1873)

Born in Brechin, the son of a merchant, Guthrie entered Edinburgh University at the early age of twelve. Having refused to renounce his evangelical convictions in order to obtain a parish, he travelled abroad and studied medicine and social conditions in Paris. In 1830 he obtained the living of Arbirlot (in Forfarshire, now Angus) and in 1837 he moved to Old Greyfriars Church, Edinburgh. At the time of the Disruption in 1843 he became the minister of Free St John's until 1864, (now St Columba's Free Church). He raised the immense sum of £116,000 in just eleven months to build manses for the new church. The poverty he found in Edinburgh prompted him to initiate important social reforms including free schooling for children and a system of district home visitors. He used his medical knowledge for the benefit of his parishioners. Guthrie started a savings bank for his people on the model of that established by Dr Henry Duncan in Ruthwell. It was reckoned that 30,000 people gathered for his funeral in Edinburgh. He is buried in the Grange Cemetery in Edinburgh.

Above: Thomas Guthrie's monument in Princes Street

Right: Memorial of Thomas Guthrie in the vestibule of St Columba's Free Church, Edinburgh

suddenly snapped and he came down on his back with a tremendous thud. He had to be carried into the manse and could do nothing for several days. Guthrie reckoned that McCheyne never fully recovered.

Anyone looking today at McCheyne's schedule of activities would have to say that he was not only extremely busy but that he did not spare himself, resulting in excessive pressure upon his physical constitution. A remarkable volume of personal correspondence, far more than his correspondents could have expected, took up much of his time.

The shadow of the Great Disruption

A number of demanding activities came together and competed for his attention and energy at this period. Throughout the years of the revival and immediately afterwards, he was engaged in the affairs of the Church of Scotland as it faced the possibility of the Disruption. He was never absent from denominational meetings at which his presence was expected. On 17 November 1842 500 ministers met in Edinburgh from all parts of Scotland. Few if any of them ever forgot hearing McCheyne's participation in their times of prayer when he 'poured out our wants before the Lord'. Ever since the Reformation the Church of Scotland had maintained her independence from the State in all spiritual matters. The issue was the spiritual independence of the churches to call their own ministers, a battle against Erastianism. 'The trials of the

Church are near,' McCheyne wrote to Horatius Bonar. 'May we be kept in the shadow of the Rock.' Two months after his death the matter was decided, contrary to what he and his colleagues had urged.

However, the revival continued in St Peter's and throughout Scotland. In September 1840 McCheyne wrote to William Burns: 'There have been evident tokens of the presence of the Spirit of God among my dear people many nights—more, I think, upon the Thursday nights than on the Sabbaths. Some I have met with seemingly awakened without any direct means. A good number of young mill-girls are still weeping after the Lord Jesus.' The counselling and nurturing of new Christians was time-consuming. At the same time invitations to preach came as the flame of revival continued. In the

Above: The first General Assembly of the Free Church of Scotland in 1843 at the time of the Disruption. Taking 23 years to complete, this is believed to be one of the first works of art painted with the help of a camera

Erastianism and the Disruption

The name originated with Thomas Erastus (1534–83), a Swiss-German theologian and opponent of Calvinism, who maintained that the church should not have the power to exclude or excommunicate people as a punishment for sin. The title Erastianism then emerged in England in the Westminster Assembly (1643) when some urged the supremacy of the state over the church, although their arguments were rejected. The point at issue in 1843 was the power of lay patrons, rather than the congregations themselves, to appoint ministers. On the 18 May 1843, 451 ministers of the Church of Scotland left its General Assembly in Edinburgh and formed the Free Church of Scotland. This meant considerable sacrifice, because many had to leave their manses and churches and they met in the open air or in tents and barns. In Dundee ten of the thirteen ministers joined in the secession to cast in their lot with the Free Church, and ten new places of worship were erected there within a few years. Had he lived, McCheyne would doubtless have been among them.

THE ACT OF SEPARATION AND DEED OF DEMISSION AT TANFIELD, EDINBURGH, MAY 1843

same month of September he wrote, 'I have been in Strathbogie also, and seen some of the Lord's wonders there.' In October 1840 he wrote again, 'God is still working here, and I look for far greater things. I am very anxious to know how I could do more good to many people and to the whole world; and not to know only but to do it.' The last recorded case of awakening—the last entry in his diary—is mentioned on January 6 1843: 'Heard of an awakened soul finding rest—true rest, I trust. Two new cases of awakening; both very deep and touching. At the very time when I was beginning to give up in despair, God gives me tokens of His presence returning.' His mention of despair was prompted by his conviction that a faithful minister ought to see conversions constantly and any absence of this blessing concerned him.

Perhaps the greatest challenge and physical demands came from his preaching excursions away from Dundee. This seems to have been his overwhelming commitment and preoccupation. 1842 was especially demanding in this respect, although in the August of that year he paid a happy visit to Clarencefield near Ruthwell and was able to spend some time with his cousins. They made no Christian profession and were hostile to evangelical Christianity. But McCheyne completely surprised them and won their confidence. They enjoyed talking with him and went with him on some of his visits to cottages where he prayed and talked with people. All three girls became earnest Christians as a result. In the October of that year they were present at St Peter's for one of the communion weekends, something that must have been a great encouragement to McCheyne and his mother, the girls' aunt.

In the summer of 1842, together with a number of ministers from Scotland, McCheyne was invited to visit the north of England to preach. The principal town was Newcastle where Burns had been preaching with considerable blessing. Besides preaching in Presbyterian and Wesleyan Methodist churches, they preached in the open air, principally in the market place. On one occasion McCheyne preached by the light of the moon to more than a thousand people between the Cloth Market and St Nicholas' church. As he finished speaking he told them 'that they would never meet again till they all met at the judgment seat of Christ.' On the way back home he preached with power at Gilsland, near Carlisle, a village directly on the course of Hadrian's Wall, and then returned to Dundee in September through his favourite part of Scotland, Dumfriesshire.

In spite of this extensive travelling McCheyne testified to his people that he had come back home refreshed and full of peace and joy. 'I have returned much stronger, indeed quite well. I think I have got some precious souls for my hire on my way home. I earnestly long for more grace and personal holiness, and more usefulness.' But soon he was off again, this time to London to assist his friend James Hamilton at his communion season at the

Above: The Cathedral Church of St Nicholas, Newcastle

Left: The remains of the church in Auchterarder, the church around which the disruption debates began

National Scotch Church in Regent Square. His flock began to murmur at his absence and McCheyne wondered again if God was calling him to an evangelistic ministry rather than a pastoral one.

The preaching activity continued in 1843 with his last evangelistic tour in February. McCheyne was appointed by the Committee of the Convocation of the Church of Scotland to visit the districts of Deer and Ellon, places where evangelical truth was not predominant in the church and where there would not have been much sympathy for the thought of the imminent Disruption. Within a period of three weeks he preached or spoke at twenty-four places, sometimes more than once in the same place. He preached in large towns like Aberdeen and Peterhead and small places like Crechie, Clola, Brucklay, New Deer and Pitsligo. He wrote, 'Tomorrow we trust to be in Aberdour; and then we leave for the Presbytery of Ellon. The weather has been delightful till now. Today the snow is beginning to drift. But God is with us, and He will carry us to the very end. I am quite well, though a little fatigued sometimes.'

'I expect a sudden call'

A letter from Dundee on 20 February reported the typhus fever still prevalent. Typhus was rife amongst the working class in the 19th century, although all the population was vulnerable to it. On 24 February he wrote, 'Today is the first day we have rested since leaving home, so that I am almost overcome with fatigue.' The trip was not without opposition. On one occasion a mob gathered intent on stoning him as soon as he began to speak, but his manner, looks and words so held their complete attention that they ended up begging him to stay and preach to them. McCheyne's response to opposition was positive: 'I can say with Paul that I have preached the Gospel from Jerusalem round about unto Illyricum, and no power on earth shall keep me from preaching it in the dead parishes of Scotland.'

McCheyne's diary is full of names of places he visited. For example, on December 13 1842, 'I preach at Newtyle tonight, and tomorrow evening at Lintrathen in a barn, and on Thursday at Kirriemuir.' Although these were only distances of 11 and 25 miles (18 and 41 kilometres) they were demanding journeys in the course of one week. If we ask why he was not easier on himself and less demanding, one answer must be that he had an awareness, sometimes expressed, that his time was short. In November 1842 he wrote, 'I do not expect to live long. I expect a sudden call some day perhaps soon, and therefore I speak very plainly.' His earnest desire for the salvation of souls motivated him. At least one member of St Peter's sensed McCheyne's awareness that his life was drawing to a close and felt he became increasingly earnest in his preaching.

The end of the road
On his return home from preaching, instead of resting he

Above: Clarencefield Cottage, close by Ruthwell, the home of McCheyne's aunt that he loved to visit both as a boy and an adult. In 1842 his visit gave him opportunity to witness to three of his cousins who became earnest Christians as a result

Above: McCheyne's grave at St Peter's in Dundee

was found going in and out among his flock, filling up every moment in pastoral visitation as well as preaching usually three times on a Sunday. The visiting of the congregation presented a particular danger as typhus fever was rampant in the parish and many whom he visited were affected by it. Much of his time was spent visiting the dying and burying the dead. He continued to preach at least twice on a Sunday to his own flock and often in the evening at Broughty Ferry near by.

One Tuesday, having spent time visiting at the east end of Dundee, he visited a friend on his way home and shared his apprehension that he had caught typhus fever in the course of his visits to fever patients in the parish. The next day he was so ill that he wondered if he would get through the night. He could only speak with difficulty and had severe head pains. Having been so frequently subject to bouts of illness, no serious alarm was felt and his sudden death on Saturday, 25 March 1843 took everyone by surprise. The *Dundee Advertiser* declared that his premature death 'created a sensation in the town, especially amongst those who sat under his ministry'. The parish register records that the cause of his death was typhus fever. He was just twenty-nine years of age. The early death of Robert Murray

McCheyne needs to be seen in the context of a particularly unhealthy environment. A basic sewage disposal system and domestic water supply were slow in reaching Dundee. Water caddies brought as much as 1000 gallons of water into the town each day, selling it for a penny for ten gallons. But this means of transport was open to infection. In 1863 the average lifespan of a man living in Dundee was only 33.

As soon as Andrew Bonar heard the news, he travelled to Dundee, aware that he could do little, but feeling compelled in spirit to go. He found McCheyne's flock gathered in the church in a state of shock and sorrow. 'Hundreds were there, the lower part of the church was full: and none among them seemed to be able to contain their sorrow. Every heart seemed bursting with grief, so that the weeping and the cries could be heard afar off.'

It was at first arranged by McCheyne's family that he should be buried in Edinburgh, but the members of St Peter's were so energetically opposed to the idea that it was abandoned in favour of Dundee. Andrew Bonar was asked to conduct the funeral on 30 March. Business almost stopped in the parish. The funeral procession was followed by nearly every man in the parish and congregation, together with members of the Dundee Presbytery, many ministers from the surrounding area, a great body of elders, most of the dissenting or non-conformist ministers in the town—and many more besides. The streets were crowded and people looked out of every window. Over six thousand attended as McCheyne was buried

Right: McCheyne's mother

a deputy, after a long days ride.

Above: McCheyne's drawing of Andrew Bonar on one of their shared journeys. The caption reads 'A deputy after a long days ride.'

in St Peter's graveyard on the pathway at the northwest corner.

McCheyne's remarkable influence

In the final analysis, the reason for McCheyne's influence upon his contemporaries must be attributed to God's sovereign purpose. But we can discern some obvious reasons that were all part of that purpose. He was known for his leadership. It seems to have been natural for him to take a lead and to be always suggesting a way forward. This was all the more

impressive because of his comparative youth. That he died so young having achieved so much is a further reason for his influence. The remarkable success of the Dundee experiment in church extension at St Peter's also increased attention because of widespread interest in the subject.

It is impossible to read the history of the period and the biographies of his contemporaries, without recognising the lasting impact he had upon them. His fellow ministers testified that they had a sense of well-being if their suggestions and ideas met with his approval. Not a year passed in Andrew Bonar's journal without him referring to McCheyne on the anniversary of his death. The experience McCheyne had of revival and all that he wrote about it stirred up considerable interest in Scotland and beyond. The biography Andrew Bonar wrote has become a Christian classic, even though its language is now somewhat dated. Many of his sermons have been published and continue to be republished, together with a great deal of his general correspondence and pastoral letters. His role model as a pastor still challenges and instructs contemporary pastors and teachers.

What is most outstanding, and probably the principal reason why his influence continues, is what can only be described as his personal holiness. To this so many writers and biographers gave unsolicited and unexpected testimony.

In recording his death even the *Dundee Advertiser* commented that 'He never for a moment assumed the character of a violent or intolerant leader, but rather trusted his advocacy to the guidance of a meek and gentle spirit, thoroughly imbued with the truth of the doctrines he so zealously taught.' Another Dundee paper, the *Dundee Warder*–a paper into which McCheyne had entered into correspondence–spoke tellingly of

Right: St Andrew's Free, Auchterarder built in 1843 as a result of the disruption, now a furniture shop

Above: The National Scotch Church in Regent Square, London

his Christ-centred character: 'Every note from his hand had a lasting interest about it; for his mind was so full of Christ, that, even in writing about the most ordinary affairs, he contrived, by some natural turn, to introduce the glorious subject that was always uppermost with him.

Thomas Guthrie wrote in his autobiography of how he remembered 'Dr Andrew Anderson of Morpeth telling me how, when he was minister of St Fergus, which he left at the Disruption, McCheyne had spent a day or two in his manse; and not only while he was there, but for a week or two after he had left, it seemed a heavenlier place than ever before. Associated with McCheyne's person, appearance and conversation, on the walls of the house and everything around

Above: One of McCheyne's elders, William Lamb

Above: *Andrew Bonar at the age of eighty*

seemed to be inscribed, "Holiness unto the Lord."'

Few knew McCheyne better than his close friend Andrew Bonar, and Bonar said that of him: 'Some felt, not so much his words, as his presence and holy solemnity, as if one spoke to them who was standing in the presence of God; and to others his prayers appeared like the breathings of one already within the veil.' McCheyne often visited Andrew Bonar at Collace and a domestic servant commented on family prayers when he was there: 'Oh, to hear Mr M'Cheyne at prayers in the mornin'! It was as if he would never gi'e ower; he had sae muckle to ask. Ye would ha'e thocht the very walls would speak again.' After McCheyne's death a letter was found in his desk from a stranger who had visited St Peter's in which he wrote, 'It was not what you said, nor even how you said it, but it was your look—it was so Christ-like—the face of one shining from being in the presence of the Lord.'

One of the reasons our hearts

McCheyne's Bible Reading Calendar

The plan takes the user through the New Testament and Psalms twice, and the rest of the Old Testament once, each year. If that seems too ambitious, the same plan can be used over a two-year cycle. It continues to be used throughout the world. In the United Kingdom the *Banner of Truth* reckons that they have sold a minimum of 155,000. UCCF have probably distributed around 55,000 from the UK since 2003 and InterVarsity/USA circulates their own edition. It is to be distributed shortly in Arabic, and Francophone Africans have similar plans. Numbers cannot be calculated because liberty is given for people to reproduce it without seeking permission. The IVP edition, available through bookshops, is ISBN 1–899464 02 6 (UK only) and 1–899464 03 4 (rest of the world). The IFES (the International Fellowship of Evangelical Students) publish it and in Rwanda they held a student conference in December 2005 called 'Raising an Ezra Generation: back to the Bible' and they requested 1,000 plans to be shipped over since students at the conference had covenanted to read the Bible through using McCheyne's plan'. The completely unknown factor is the number of people who have downloaded the programme from the web where it is freely available.

MORE PRECIOUS THAN GOLD

READ THE BIBLE IN ONE OR TWO YEARS

IFES

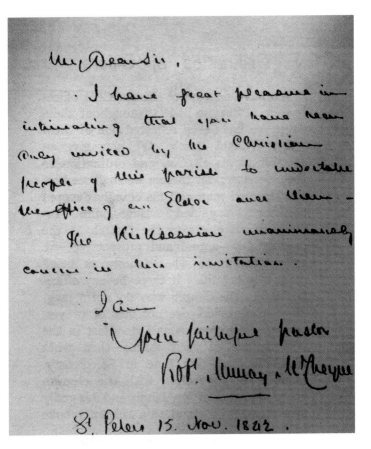

Above: The letter of invitation to William Lamb from McCheyne to become an elder

respond so readily to McCheyne as we read of him is that while he was a Presbyterian he was wide in his sympathies. He was glad to have evangelical preachers from other denominations preach at St Peter's, and he was warm in his regard for all who loved the Lord Jesus Christ and the gospel. McCheyne was happy to enter into association with all agencies that furthered the truth of the gospel and reached out to society. He believed it 'to be the mind of Christ, that all who are true servants of the Lord Jesus Christ, sound in the faith, called to the ministry, and owned of God therein, should love one another, pray one for another, bid one another God-speed, own one another as fellow-soldiers, fellow-servants, and fellow-labourers in the vineyard, and, so far as God offereth opportunity, help one another in the work of the ministry.'

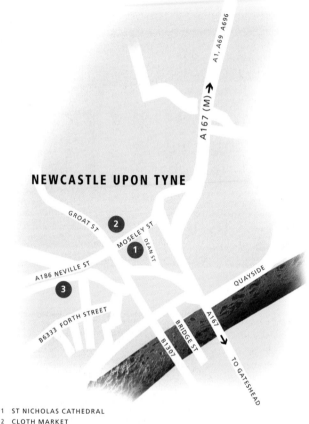

NEWCASTLE UPON TYNE

1 ST NICHOLAS CATHEDRAL
2 CLOTH MARKET
3 STATION

TRAVEL INFORMATION

St Nicolas Cathedral, Newcastle

St Nicholas is now the Cathedral church of Newcastle, located at the junction of Mosley Street, Collingwood Street and St Nicholas Street, at the south end of the Groat Market. There has been a church on this site for over 900 years although nothing now remains of the original buildings. The present church dates from the 14th and 15th centuries. Originally the parish church of the town of Newcastle upon Tyne, St Nicholas church became a cathedral in 1882 when the new diocese of Newcastle was created out of the northern part of the diocese of Durham. (www.newcastle-ang-cathedral-stnicholas.org.uk).

Dundee

Camperdown House, located in Camperdown Country Park

Built in 1828 and designed by the architect William Burn, it was

Above: *Camperdown House, Dundee*

named after the Battle of Camperdown, where Admiral Adam Duncan triumphed over the Dutch fleet in 1797. The Duncan family used the pensions granted by a grateful British government, to build this magnificent house. The City of Dundee Council now own the house and park, and the ground-floor rooms of the house have been restored and contain displays relating to Dundee's maritime history, Admiral Duncan and the Battle of Camperdown. (www.camperdownpark. com).

Above: *St Columba's Free Church, Edinburgh, formed in 1843 at the Disruption and opened in 1845 as Free St John's, with Thomas Guthrie as its first minister and called St Columba's when it joined with Fountainbridge Free Church after 1900*

Above: McCheyne's Dundee: Dundee New Exchange and Shipping
Below: Tay Road Bridge under construction in 1964

For further reading

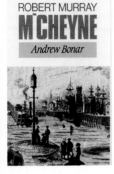

Andrew Bonar, *Memoir and Remains of Robert Murray McCheyne* (London: Banner of Truth, 1964).

Andrew Bonar, *The Life of Rev. Robert Murray McCheyne* (London: Banner of Truth, 1972).

David Robertson, *Awakening—The Life and Ministry of Robert Murray McCheyne* (Carlisle: Paternoster 2004).

L.J. Van Valen, *Constrained by His Love* (Fearn, Tain: Christian Focus 2002).

Two Collections of McCheyne's Sermons: *From the Preacher's Heart* (Fearn, Tain: Christian Focus, 1993) and *A Basket of Fragments* (Fearn, Tain: Christian Focus, 1979) .

About the author

After serving churches in the UK as a pastor for a total of thirty years—first at Lansdowne Evangelical Free Church, West Norwood, in London and then at Charlotte Chapel in Edinburgh—Derek Prime has devoted himself since 1987 to an itinerant ministry and to writing. Derek is married to Betty.

A summary of Robert Murray McCheyne's life

21 May 1813	Born in Edinburgh
1818	Started at the English School in Edinburgh
1821–1827	Pupil at the High School, Edinburgh
1827	Entered Edinburgh University at the age of fourteen
1829	Became a member of St Stephen's Church, Edinburgh
8 July 1831	Death of his brother David
1831	The year probably of McCheyne's conversion
28 September 1831	Presented himself to the Church of Scotland Edinburgh Presbytery as a candidate for the ministry. He was examined and allowed to proceed with theological training in the winter
18 November 1834	Wrote the hymn 'Jehovah Tsidkenu'—'I once was a stranger to grace and to God'
16 February 1835	Preached a trial sermon before his professors
29 March 1835	His last day at divinity hall
30 June 1835	Licensed by the presbytery of Annan
1 July 1835	First sermons preached at Ruthwell on the day following his licensing
7 November 1835	He began his work as an assistant at Larbert
April 13 1836	Together with Alexander Somerville, Robert spent time with Alexander Duff home from India
14 August 1836	Invited to preach at a new church in Dundee, St Peter's, as a possible candidate
24 November 1836	Ordained and inducted to the charge of St Peter's Church, Dundee
1838	Church of Scotland's General Assembly's decision to appoint a committee to examine the state and condition of the Jewish people

20 September 1838	Andrew Bonar inducted at Collace
1838 towards its end	McCheyne's ill health meant spending time at his parents' home in Edinburgh
1839	Expedition to Palestine
27 March 1839	The beginning of the deputation to Israel's journey as they sailed for London
9 April 1839	Farewell Service at Regent Square Church, London
12 April 1839	Deputation left Dover for France
7 June 1839	Jerusalem came within sight
15 June 1839	They received the first letters from home since their departure with the news that the Auchterarder case had been decided against the Church in the House of Lords
8 August 1839	The beginning of the revival at St Peter's Church, Dundee
July 1840	McCheyne went to Ireland and spoke in Belfast and Dublin about the Church's responsibilities for the Jews
December 1842	He devised his yearly calendar for his people, reading the Old Testament once and the New Testament and Psalms twice.
1842 autumn	Visited the north of England on an evangelistic mission and other journeys to London and Aberdeenshire
1843	In 1843 McCheyne was appointed to be a commissioner to the General Assembly, an Assembly that was to result in the Disruption and the establishment of the Free Church of Scotland.
12 March 1843	Preached his last sermon at St Peter's
25 March 1843	Death aged 29
1844	Publication of *Memoir and Remains of Robert Murray McCheyne*

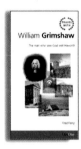

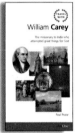

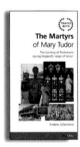

**TITLES IN THE SERIES:
128 PAGES £10 EACH**

JOHN BUNYAN

ISBN 978 1 903087 12 1,
REF: TWJB 121

CH SPURGEON

ISBN 978 903087 11 4,
REF: TWCS 114

WILLIAM BOOTH

ISBN 978 1 903087 35 X,
REF: TWWB 35X

JOHN KNOX

ISBN 978 1 903087 350,
REF TWJK 350

WILLIAM GRIMSHAW

ISBN 978 1 903087 68 8,
REF: TWWG 688

THE BRITISH MUSEUM

ISBN 978 1 903087 54 1,
REF: TBM 541

MARTYN LLOYD-JONES

ISBN 978 1 903087 58 9,
REF: TWMLJ 589

WILLIAM CAREY

ISBN 978 1 903087 76 3,
REF: TWWC 763

**MARTYRS OF
MARY TUDOR**

ISBN 978 1 842625 0033,
REF:TWMM 033

WILLIAM WILBERFORCE

ISBN 978 1 842625 027 9,
REF:TWMM 279

CS LEWIS

ISBN 978 1 84625 056 9,
REF:TWCSL 569

**ROBERT MURRAY
McCHEYNE**

ISBN 978 1 84625 0576
REF:TWRMM 576